Rosemary Moon's

ice cream
machine book

Rosemary Moon's
ice cream
machine book

Frozen delights to prepare —
home-made ice creams, sherbets, sorbets,
frozen yoghurts, and desserts

APPLE

This book is for Kate Bishop, who won an
ice-cream machine and has never looked back since.

A QUINTET BOOK

Published by Apple Press
Sheridan House
112-116A Western Road
Hove
East Sussex BN3 1DD

ISBN 1-84092-317-2

Reprinted in 2000, 2001, 2002

This book was designed and produced by
Quintet Publishing Limited
6 Blundell Street
London N7 9BH

Creative Director: Richard Dewing
Art Director: Silke Braun
Design: Balley Design Associates
Simon Balley & Joanna Hill
Project Editor: Diana Steedman
Editor: Lisa Cussans
Photographer: Andrew Sydenham
Food Stylist: Jennie Berresford

Typeset in Great Britain by Central Southern Typesetters, Eastbourne
Manufactured in Singapore by Eray Scan Pte Ltd
Printed in Singapore by Star Standard Industries (Pte) Ltd

The recipes in this book have been compiled for
use in a variety of ice cream machines, or indeed without a machine at all.
Always refer to your manufacturer's instructions regarding capacity and operation.

CONTENTS

Introduction

Making ice cream at home must be one of the most creative and utterly indulgent forms of cooking there is. In the old days, ice-cream making was a bore, since it was necessary to take the mixture out of the freezer two, three or more times during the freezing process in order to beat it vigorously, an essential labour to ensure the finished confection was not full of ice crystals.

Nowadays, ice-cream making couldn't be easier, following the advent of the domestic ice-cream machine. These come in all shapes and sizes, bearing a startling range of price tags, but all transform the actual freezing and mixing, or churning, of ice creams into a quick and simple job. This book shows how to make a selection of ice creams, sorbets and other frozen desserts with the minimum of fuss and effort, using an ice-cream machine to do the tedious work. Take away the effort, and preparing ice creams is almost as much fun as eating them!

An Internationally Popular Food

Ice cream is one of the world's most popular foods. It is a firm favourite with children, and a sophisticated, seductive and satisfying confection for the rest of us. If there are Seven Ages of Man, then ice cream is pretty much a perfect food for all of them.

The international perception of ice cream has changed dramatically during the last decade of the 20th century. The discerning shopper wants to buy products made from "real" ingredients, so there has been a tremendous move towards "old-fashioned" ice creams made with milk or cream, eggs and pure flavourings. The designer commercial ice creams now available are exceptional in flavour and texture but, more than ever before, you get what you pay for. The luxury product comes with luxury price tag.

Making ice cream at home is not an economical process. I believe there is no point in embarking on the preparation of an ice cream if you are not going to produce an even better result than the best products available in the shops. To do this you must use the best ingredients: the freshest eggs and cream or milk, ripe, unblemished fruits, quality flavourings and the finest chocolate, coffee and nuts.

This book is about luxury and indulgence, but it also has a conscience, and so includes a delicious selection of recipes for reduced-fat ice creams and ices. Whether you are addicted to rich ice creams, Italian gelatos, sorbets or ice milks, you will find recipes here to tempt and titillate. I hope you will discover not only new ideas for flavours, but also styles of ice creams and ices you may not have tried before— lightly creamy sherbets and wonderful frozen yogurts. I hope that you enjoy them all as much as I have.

There are two types of home ice-cream makers: those that have to be prefrozen in advance and then kept in the freezer and those that contain their own compressor or freezer unit. Both are basically a container in which the ice is frozen, with a dasher, or paddle, inserted into it to churn the mixture during freezing. This prevents the formation of ice crystals and introduces air, to give a lighter texture to the finished ice cream. The continuous action of the dasher during freezing means that manual beating is unnecessary, unless you wish to incorporate extra ingredients just before serving.

poured into the bucket after the dasher and motor unit, housed in the lid of the machine, have been clipped into place. The ice cream is churned on the countertop. Similar machines have been available to churn actually in the freezer, although these are now less common than the countertop variety.

Other bucket machines that must be hand cranked are also available but require much more effort on behalf of the operator. Very small sizes are fun for children but I reckon anyone making ice cream should make enough for the whole family.

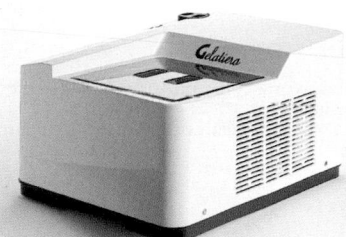

Freezer-assisted Machines

The machines that must be used in the freezer are simply double-skinned buckets containing refrigerant, which must be frozen before the ice-cream maker can be used. This may take up to eight hours, so it is necessary to keep the bucket in the freezer if you intend to make ice cream regularly or on the spur of the moment. The obvious disadvantage is that the bucket takes up a considerable amount of freezer storage space, one thing few of us can afford to sacrifice.

To use the machine, the ice-cream or sorbet mix is

Countertop Machines

The ideal is an ice-cream maker that comes with its own freezer unit. I suppose their main disadvantage, other than an inflated price tag, is the amount of storage space they take up, either countertop or in a cupboard. Some countertop models may be prefrozen for up to five minutes (a vast improvement on the six to eight hours recommended for prefreezing the bucket-type machine) before adding the prepared mixture. The dasher is either driven by a motor on the lid, or from within the body of the machine. I have found that the latter generally gives the best results, as the motor is less likely to labour during the final stages of freeze-churning.

If you are lucky enough to own a countertop machine, I recommend you keep it out, if possible. The freezer unit will not take kindly to being tipped to get the machine in and out of cupboards.

Cleaning

All domestic ice-cream machines are difficult to clean, especially the countertop models, since the bucket should not be immersed in water. The ice cream must therefore be scooped out of the bucket, and then the machine cleaned *in situ*. I generally wipe mine out with a hot, soapy dishcloth, wringing it out several times in clean water, and then wipe the machine down with kitchen paper. After several uses I wipe it round with a sterilizing solution—the type used for babies' bottles is fine. Most of the dashers and lids can be put in a dishwasher but always check your instruction book before doing so.

The larger countertop machines are supplied with a removable bucket of a slightly smaller capacity than the main machine. This makes cleaning much easier but you may find the reduced capacity a problem. The space between the inner and fixed buckets must be filled with a suitable conductor before use, or the refrigeration process will be hampered. A salt solution or some alcohol should be used—an excellent way of using up the dregs in bottles or the neighbours' home-made offerings. Some people recommend vodka as the best conductor, but what a waste! I'd much rather have the larger quantities of ice cream!

MACHINE CAPACITIES

Most domestic machines have a capacity of either 425 ml/15 fl oz or 850 ml/1½ pints. It is essential that you check the capacity of your machine before using the following recipes, all of which are written for a 850 ml/1½ pint machine. Remember that you should get more out of your machine than you put in, because one of the prime purposes of the dasher is to introduce air into the mixture while churning. For this reason, you should never fill the bucket of your machine to more than half or two-thirds full.

Always remember that there is little point in making ice cream at home unless it is going to be better than the best the shops have to offer. To achieve this, you must use the very finest ingredients possible. Fresh is not only best, it is essential for making really luscious ice creams that will last, given a chance, for up to two months in the freezer. This is particularly important for eggs, milk and cream.

Milk

Whole milk is best, producing a smooth frozen dessert that is less likely to fill with ice crystals during storage. A certain amount of fat is necessary in most ice creams, unless they are meant to be granular, as is the case with some sorbets. Semi-skimmed or skimmed milks should only be used for ice milks and other low-fat ices, to be eaten immediately after freeze-churning.

Cream

Two types of cream are used in these recipes. Single cream makes the richest of custards for delicious, French-style ice creams. It can also be added to sherbets, and may be incorporated into frozen yogurt or other mixtures where some light richness is called for to enhance the texture.

When adding cream to ice creams and frozen yogurts just before churning, use double cream. In an ice cream, I have a simple rule of thumb: if the custard has been made with milk, I add the double cream without whipping it. If the custard was made with single cream, I lightly whip the double cream before folding it into the custard—just until it is thick and floppy but not stiff.

Yogurt

I do not use a live or cultured yogurt in these recipes, avoiding the introduction of any bacteria or enzymes, even the good ones! I use a standard pasteurized, runny, natural yogurt for all the recipes, although you may like to try the luxury frozen yogurts with a slightly sweetened creamy variety. Greek-style yogurt will make luscious frozen yogurts, but they may be slightly thicker and heavier than those made with a regular variety.

Eggs

These should be as fresh as possible. I have used large eggs throughout this book. Many ice creams contain raw egg white, but the yolks are usually cooked lightly to thicken a custard mixture. Do not use eggs with cracked shells, which may be liable to bacterial infection. It is recommended that expectant mothers should not eat raw eggs.

Dried Egg And Egg Substitutes

Anyone concerned about the safety of raw eggs may like to make their ice cream with a dried egg product, such as those available for cake decorating. Follow the instructions on the packet to reconstitute the egg. I haven't actually made ice cream with dried egg, but there is no reason for it not to work.

Sugars

In most of my recipes I use caster sugar, as it dissolves quickly and keeps a pure colour in the mixture. With chocolate ice creams you may prefer to use a raw cane sugar or a light muscavado. I use demerara sugar in coffee ice creams. There are no hard and fast rules, but remember that different sugars have different strengths of sweetness, and you may have to adjust the quantity slightly.

Too much sugar will overwhelm the ice cream mixture and affect the freezing; if you have gone seriously overboard on the sweetness scale, the ice cream may never freeze but remain slushy and sticky. And don't be tempted to reduce the calories in an ice cream by adding too little sugar, since this can cause the frozen mixture to be very hard and granular, or to crumble during storage.

Honey

This natural sweetener is actually less sweet than sugar, but has a very distinctive taste. I generally use it as a flavouring, and not as the main sweetening agent. Like sugar, if you use too much the freezing of the ice cream will be affected. Use honey in a liquid state, which makes it easier to blend into the other ingredients. If you want to use a particular set honey, perhaps because of its flavour, melt the required amount of honey, either over a pan of hot water or in a microwave, before adding it to the other ingredients.

Golden Syrup And Maple Syrup

Although these syrups are sweet, they are not used as the main sweetener in ice cream since their liquid state would affect the balance and texture. Golden and maple syrups also have a fairly delicate flavour, and a more intense sweetener is generally required. Golden syrup is often added to commercial reduced-fat sorbets and ice creams to give more texture and body to the mix, but I use these syrups more as a flavouring for sauces and ripples, rather than in the main ice-cream mix.

Liqueurs And Alcohol

These can make a world of difference to the flavour of a finished ice cream, but if you are by nature a generous host, you will have to learn to master your generosity or the freezing characteristics of your frozen dessert

will be changed completely by too much alcohol! It slows the freezing right down, so the more you add, the longer you will have to wait to eat the finished product.

Fresh Fruits

These should always be in peak condition. Underripe fruits have little flavour (though a spoonful of a complimentary liqueur will help), while overripe fruits deteriorate quickly, even when frozen, affecting the quality of the ice cream and tarnishing it with a musty flavour.

Dried Fruits

Choose those with the best and brightest flavours; sun-dried apricots, for example, have a natural sweetness not always found in those dried by other methods.

Nuts

These should be as fresh as possible. Most nuts contain a large amount of oil, which can quickly turn rancid and spoil the flavour of the kernels. I always recommend buying in small quantities, and using them up quickly. Store nuts in a cool, dark place, and not in a jar in a bright, sunny kitchen.

Chocolate

The quality of chocolate varies enormously, and the only guide you can rely on is the amount of cocoa solids in each bar. The ideal for a good, dark quality

bar is 70 per cent. I like to cut my own chocolate chips for ice cream from a good bar of chocolate; they taste better than the commercial ones, and the irregular shapes add extra textural interest to the ice cream. Always use cocoa powder and not drinking chocolate in these recipes; the latter is often sweetened and will upset the final flavour balance. Dutch cocoa is one of the best, if you can find it.

Vanilla

This is probably the most basic ice-cream flavouring in the world, and certainly one of the most popular. I prefer to use vanilla extract as a liquid vanilla; it is strong, with a gloriously pure flavour. This is just what you would expect from a product so much more expensive than vanilla essence, which has just a little vanilla mixed with a synthetic flavouring.

Vanilla pods give the best vanilla flavouring of all. They are infused (immersed and left to steep) either with milk or cream, and then washed thoroughly for later use. For extra-rich vanilla ice cream, I split the pods with a sharp knife and scrape out the tiny black seeds, which I then add for extra flavour just before churning (split and scraped vanilla pods should then be discarded, or may be used to flavour sugar; don't use again for cooking purposes). The best vanilla pods and extract come from Madagascar.

Coffee

Coffee ice creams are among my favourites, but I like their flavour to be robust, much as I like my coffee. To achieve this, I always grind my own beans, and use a strong or high roast blend. It is essential to use a coarse grind, which will allow you to sieve the infused mixture and remove all the grounds. I find that filter coffee often leaves very fine sediment in an ice cream, which can spoil its texture.

For some Italian-style ice creams I use instant espresso coffee, which dissolves into the mixture very easily and gives quite an authentic flavour.

When An Ice Cream Isn't

To be strictly correct, essentially in terms of commercial or shop-bought ice creams, a product to be sold as an ice cream must contain between 10–20 per cent fat. In broad terms, the ice creams at the lower end of the fat scale are economy products, usually fairly light and often artificially flavoured. Those at the opposite end are the luxury or designer ice creams, the ones with expensive supporting advertising and a very high quality image. They usually contain large chunks of added ingredients: fruits, fudge, chocolate chips or cookie dough, and are also made with natural flavourings. It is these designer products that the home ice-cream maker must aim to better.

Reduced-fat Ice Creams

True ice creams are anything but a low-fat food, though very good products can be made with a much lower fat content. These are not necessarily low calorie, however, as many still have a high proportion of sugar. Ice milks, which are little more

than frozen milk drinks, come into the reduced-fat category.

Sorbets

These are usually fruit based and have no dairy content, although some contain egg whites. They are made with a sugar syrup, and are very refreshing.

Gelatos

Gelato, or *gelati*, is the generic name for a variety of Italian ices. A *granita* is a still-frozen Italian ice, usually full of ice crystals because of its freezing method, but it is just as likely to be labelled a *gelato* as a rich Italian ice cream or a *semifreddo*, which is light and more like a sherbet. The most distinguishing characteristic of all Italian ice creams is that they have very strong, unmistakable flavours.

Frozen Yogurts And Tofu Ice Creams

Originally positioned in the health food sector of the ice-cream market, commercial frozen yogurts are usually fruity, and can be very straightforward, or luxurious with the addition of cream and eggs. Tofu, a high-protein bean curd, can be made into ice cream for those following special diets. It mixes well with soya milk, making it a good alternative ice-cream base for anyone with an allergy to traditional dairy foods.

Sherbets

Sherbets are one stage further on towards an ice cream from a sorbet. They contain some milk, buttermilk or cream, but are much lighter than a true ice cream. I think sherbets are really my favourite type of ice cream.

The Finer Points of Ice Cream Making

Completing any of the following recipes to the end of freeze-churning in your ice-cream machine is not necessarily the end of making your ice cream. You can serve most of the mixtures straight from the ice-cream maker once churning is complete, but there are occasions you may need to go a little further with preparation.

Hardening

Freshly churned ice creams are frozen, but not really solid. They are usually in a perfect state to eat straight away, but they are not always ideal for presentation. If you want to serve your ice creams and ices in scoops, you will need to harden the mixture in the freezer.

Hardening is best done by repacking the ice cream into a freezer container, so you can press the mixture down well and squeeze out any air. The actual hardening to a state suitable for long-term freezer storage may take several hours, especially if there is alcohol in the mixture, but most will be hardened ready for scooping in about two hours.

If you are really aiming to impress, you may choose to harden your ice cream slightly, then scoop it and further harden the individual scoops. This will lead to near-perfect presentation in your chosen glasses, but this book is all about having fun and enjoying your ice cream, so strike the correct balance between aesthetics and eatability.

Storage

There is a common myth that ice cream will keep in tiptop condition almost indefinitely. Certainly commercial ice creams that have added stabilizers and preservatives have a long storage life of six months or more, but designer ice creams, in common with home-made products, have a much more limited storage life.

I would not recommend keeping home-made ice cream for longer than two months if you wish to present it in perfect condition. A longer storage will lead to a deterioration in colour, flavour and texture. If you make a large batch and continually remove a few scoops from it, you will quickly find ice crystals forming on the surface, which will gradually lead to a general deterioration in the ice cream.

Ice creams and ices are best stored in good-quality plastic containers with tightly fitting lids. They should be flat and rectangular in shape, rather than deep and square. This will cause the ice to harden more quickly, and will also provide a greater surface for scooping. The containers should be filled to within 1 cm/½ in of the rim and, as with all frozen foods, each should be clearly labelled with the name of the ice cream and the date on which it was made and frozen. I suggest laying a piece of freezer or non-stick baking paper on the surface of the ice cream once it no longer fills the container, in order to help prevent ice crystals forming on the surface.

Tempering

Tempered foods are still frozen, but have softened just enough to allow for some reshaping or cutting. Frozen ices must be tempered before they are suitable for serving and eating.

Ice creams are heavier or denser than sorbets and sherbets, and require a slightly longer tempering time before they are ready to serve. I generally allow 20–30 minutes for an ice cream, and about 15 minutes for the lighter, fruitier ices. If your kitchen's temperature is very warm, I recommend you temper a batch in the refrigerator, which will give a more even result. In winter months, leave them in a cool room, away from direct sunlight and heat. Any food that is tempered or

defrosted too quickly will loose moisture and "weep," thereby changing the texture for the worse.

Making Ice Cream Without An Ice-cream Machine

This is perfectly possible, but requires much more effort as the ice cream will need to be stirred several times during freezing, to prevent large ice crystals forming in the mixture. The freezing process is also long; most will take about six hours to harden completely. You can speed the freezing process by placing the ice-cream mix in shallow containers and placing at the bottom of the freezer. The ice-cream machine has certainly made short work of this most creative and enjoyable culinary art.

Rippling

A ripple is an ice cream that has been marbled with a fruit syrup or sweet sauce, which sounds fairly simple but is more difficult in practice. Too much syrup, and the ice cream will change colour completely; too little, and it will merely assume a vaguely flecked appearance. Commercial ice-cream makers produce a ripple by pumping ice cream and syrup simultaneously into cartons and tubs, but it is very hard to achieve the same effect at home. I have found two ways that work reasonably well, but in both cases the ripple will be more effective if you chill the syrup or sauce well before adding it to the ice cream. This will help it to freeze more quickly, and therefore remain as a ripple.

Once an ice cream has been freeze-churned, it can be rippled in the ice-cream machine bucket before being hardened; when adding a sauce or syrup, you will need at least a short hardening period for the ice to set the ripple into the cream. I suggest you remove the dasher, scraping the ice cream back into the bucket and packing it down firmly. Press it down with the spatula supplied, since metal spoons will easily scratch the canister, making it less hygienic. Make four or five holes in the ice cream by poking a thin wooden spoon handle down through the mixture. Pour the sauce into the holes, and leave for about five minutes to harden slightly. The ice cream should then be scooped out of the machine into a freezer container, taking some of the sauce along with each scoop, and thereby causing a rippled effect. Pack the ice cream firmly into the container, then harden it for at least 30 minutes before serving.

A slightly more simple, but fairly effective ripple can also be achieved by scooping ice cream into a tub, as above, but then adding the sauce by spooning it over the cream in the container. As long as the sauce is evenly distributed this method will achieve satisfactory results for minimum effort, the ripple becoming apparent when the ice cream is scooped after a short hardening period.

I have tried to achieve a ripple by adding a sauce at the end of freeze-churning, mixing it into the ice cream with just a rotation or two of the dasher. The drawback of this method is that, with all the machines I have used, mixing it seems to be the operative description: the sauce or syrup just combine as one with the ice cream.

Scooping

There are two main types of ice-cream scoop: those with a spring-operated thumb-release to coax the ice cream out into the glass or cone, and those that rely on the warmth of the hand to operate a self-defrosting antifreeze sealed into the handle of the scoop, which prevents the ice cream from sticking to the metal. The latter was the ingenious invention of a Mr Zeroll of Pennsylvania in 1935, and has earned a place in numerous modern design collections.

Plastic scoops are generally less effective than those made of metal—the success is all down to the heat-conductive properties of the scoop. In commercial terms, the size of the scoop represents the number of servings it will achieve from a standard bucket of ice cream, but for domestic use a medium scoop is best; too large, and the ice cream will overflow the edges of cones and wafers, if that is your chosen method of serving.

The perfect scoop for cones can be achieved if you avoid the temptation to dig into your container of ice cream. Simply draw the scoop towards you over the surface of the ice cream until the scoop is filled, creating a well-shaped ball of ice cream. For scoops to be served as desserts on plates, and for those to be made from ice creams frozen with a smaller surface area, you may have to dig the scoop into the mixture, which will result in a scoop with a flattened base.

Real ice-cream addicts will soon find that there are all manner of accessories available, both antique and modern, to change ice-cream eating from a simple pleasure to a real ceremony.

Serving Ice Creams And Ices

Serving can be as simple or as elegant as you wish, or as you have the time to make it! A glance through the photographs in this book will start your mind racing at the presentation possibilities, but remember that the ice cream itself is the most important thing. Do not sacrifice the texture for the sake of presentation.

The most elegant presentation is made in glasses, so you can see the colour and texture of the ice cream and all its decorations. Match your spoon to the glass;

Chocolate Coating

To make the simplest of deluxe ice-cream desserts, perfect round scoops of ice cream should be returned to the freezer to harden on a baking sheet. They may then be quickly dipped in melted chocolate and briefly frozen again on greaseproof paper. Two good forks are essential for any dipping; I use general-purpose cooks' forks with long handles, but specific confectionery forks are available.

Smaller ice-cream scoops may also be rolled in chopped nuts, chocolate vermicelli or sieved cocoa powder. Really tiny scoops, which you may need to shape with teaspoons, can be coated and served as ice-cream sweets. The Savoy Hotel in London often serves ice-cream petits fours, which are borne into the dining room on platters over a bed of dry ice, billowing forth and creating a marvellous spectacle!

a short-handled teaspoon is no use at all if you are serving in very tall sundae or champagne glasses.

Chocolate and caramel decorations are the simplest. Chocolate leaves and other embellishments may be bought from cake-decorating shops and many large supermarkets, but it is better to make your own as you will be able to control the quality of the chocolate used.

Build up a collection of swizzle sticks, straws and cocktail accessories, since they can all be used for decorating ice creams. Fruity designs are great with sorbets and sherbets, and I find it really useful to have a few wacky props to hand for these fruit mixtures, which start to melt more quickly than ice creams, shortening the time available for decoration.

How To Make Basic Ice Cream

b a s i c   v a n i l l a   i c e   c r e a m

Most ice creams are made from a custard base, using either milk or cream. The secret of a successful egg custard

is to cook it slowly, so there is no risk of the eggs curdling and spoiling the texture of the finished mixture.

Vanilla ice cream may be flavoured with vanilla pods, vanilla extract, or vanilla essence.

INGREDIENTS

4 large egg yolks

75 g/2³/₄ oz caster sugar

300 ml/10 fl oz milk

1 tsp vanilla extract, or 2 tsp vanilla essence

300 ml/10 fl oz double cream

METHOD

1 Beat the egg yolks with the sugar until pale and thick. Do not use an electric beater, which will make the mixture too bubbly and frothy.

2 Warm the milk, and pour it onto the eggs, stirring continuously.

3 Rinse the milk pan in cold water; this will help to prevent the mixture from catching and sticking. Heat the custard slowly, stirring all the time, until it just coats the back of a wooden spoon in a thin film. Do not let the custard cook too quickly or the eggs will curdle. Cool the custard off the heat.

4 Stir the vanilla and the unwhipped cream into the cold custard, then chill in the fridge before freeze-churning in your ice-cream machine.

Using An Ice-Cream Machine

The bucket for these machines must be frozen well in advance of churning your ice cream.

Remove the motor unit and dasher, and place the unit in the freezer for eight hours,

or as directed in the manufacturer's instructions.

METHOD

❶ Remove the frozen bucket from the freezer, replace the dasher and clip the motor unit in place.

❷ Switch the machine on before adding the chilled custard.

❸ Pour the custard in through the feed tube while the dasher is rotating. Continue to churn until the ice cream is ready to serve, or to harden.

❹ Serve immediately, or pack into a suitable container to harden in the freezer.

TIPS

• *Always use the best and freshest ingredients possible.*

• *Never overfill your ice-cream machine.*

• *Do not use metal spoons and scrapers with your ice-cream machine as they may scratch.*

• *Read the manufacturer's instructions for your ice-cream machine.*

• *Use ice creams and ices immediately, or within two months.*

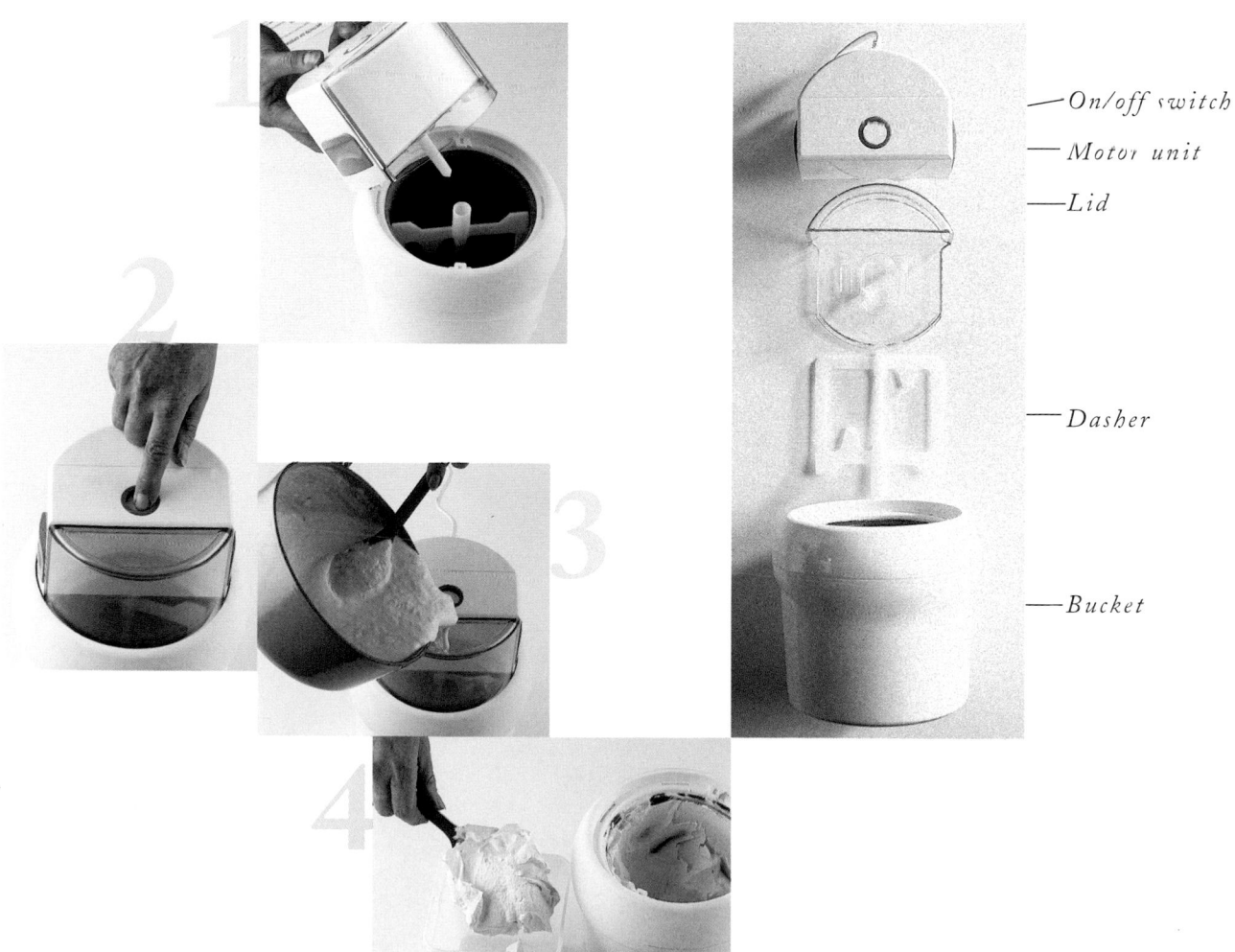

— *On/off switch*

— *Motor unit*

— *Lid*

— *Dasher*

— *Bucket*

I C E   C R E A M S

blueprint ice cream VANILLA	CHOCOLATE COOKIE
blueprint ice cream EXTRA-RICH VANILLA	ENGLISH TOFFEE
CHOCOLATE	NEW ORLEANS PRALINE
CHILLI	MOCHA ALMOND
CHOCOLATE FUDGE RIPPLE	MINT CHOCOLATE CHIP
COFFEE CREAM PECAN	CHOCOLATE COOKIE DOUGH
APPLE CINNAMON	**blueprint non-custard ice cream** STRAWBERRY
BRANDIED EGGNOG	BLACKBERRY
HONEY & CARDAMOM	PUMPKIN PIE
GINGER	LEMON & LIME
BROWN BREAD	ENGLISH PLUM & CINNAMON
PISTACHIO	CARAMEL
DOUBLE CHOC CHIP	

*M*ost of the ice-cream recipes included here are made with a rich custard base with an addition of cream just before freeze-churning.

For a custard-based ice cream, I would allow a minimum of four hours from start to finish. This is nothing to do with the length of time required to freeze-churn, it's simply that many of the mixtures require a double heating—once to flavour the milk, and then again to thicken the custard—and must then cool completely before the ice cream can be completed.

When preparing the very richest and thickest ice creams, such as the Chilli Ice Cream, I find it advisable to whip the thicker cream until floppy before folding it into the chilled custard, since it results in a lighter texture for the finished ice cream.

Some ice creams included here are made simply by adding fruit syrup or purée to whipped cream. I have included them with the ice creams because they are so deliciously creamy. When adding a large amount of fruit to whipped cream, it should be added slowly, whisking all the time, to prevent the cream from curdling.

The freeze-churning of these ice creams will take about 20–25 minutes, depending on your machine. Ice creams increase considerably during churning, since the cream traps air incorporated into the mixture by the action of the dasher. Never fill the canister of the machine by more than half before churning, or the finished mixture may overflow.

All the ice creams in this chapter may be eaten immediately after freeze-churning, straight from the ice-cream machine. They may also be hardened and stored in the freezer, and all will keep well for about two months. If stored for any longer, the flavour and texture will start to deteriorate, the texture mainly through freezer burn.

Because all these ice creams are rich and creamy, and therefore dense in texture, it will be necessary to temper, or soften, them after freezer storage before they can be served. To ensure an evenly soft texture throughout, it is best to do this in the refrigerator, allowing around 30 minutes for a full quantity of ice cream. Refreeze any remaining ice cream immediately after serving; it should not be allowed to melt before being returned to the freezer.

✔ANILLA

This is a basic ice cream which can be adapted for many different flavours, or made slightly lighter by adding

up to twice as much milk as stated. Do check the capacity of your machine before doing so.

INGREDIENTS

4 large egg yolks

75 g/2³/₄ oz caster sugar

300 ml/10 fl oz milk

1 tsp vanilla extract, or 2 tsp vanilla essence

300 ml/10 fl oz double cream

METHOD

❶ Whisk the egg yolks and sugar together until thick and pale. This is best done with a fork so that the mixture does not become too frothy, but it will take some time.

❷ Heat the milk until almost boiling then pour it onto the eggs, stirring all the time with a wooden spoon.

❸ Return the mixture to the pan and heat gently, stirring continuously, until the custard just coats the back of the spoon—do not cook for too long or the eggs will start to scramble.

❹ Leave until cold—the mixture will cool quicker if transferred to a clean bowl—then stir in the vanilla and the unbeaten cream. Chill thoroughly for at least one hour.

❺ Spoon or scrape the mixture into the ice-cream machine, then freeze-churn until ready to serve.

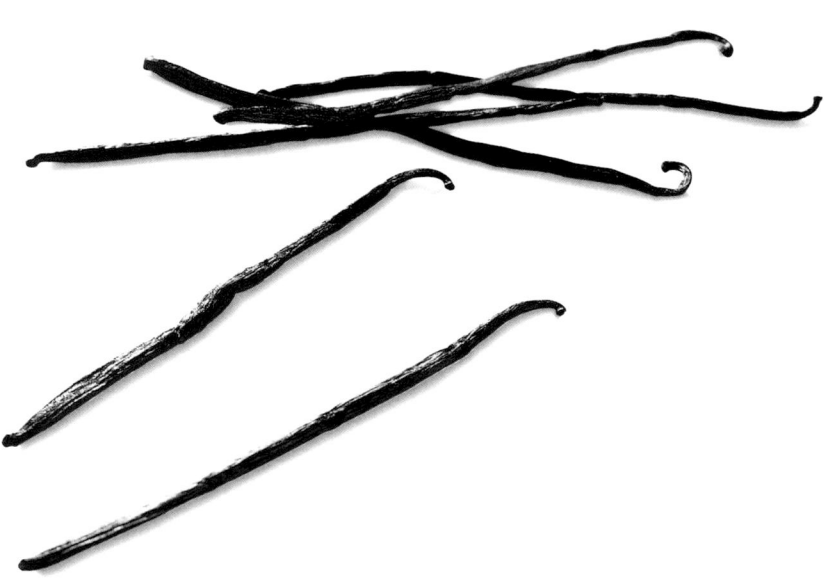

*E*XTRA-RICH *V*ANILLA

Home-made ice cream should be as creamy as possible, so this is my favourite basic recipe.

INGREDIENTS

300 ml/10 fl oz single cream

1 vanilla pod

4 large egg yolks

100 g/3½ oz caster sugar

300 ml/10 fl oz double cream

METHOD

❶ Heat the single cream with the vanilla pod until almost boiling, then remove the pan from the heat. Cover, then leave for at least 20 minutes, or until cold. Remove the vanilla pod; rinse it well, and store for future use.

❷ Whisk the egg yolks and sugar together until thick and pale, but not too frothy.

❸ Reheat the cream until almost boiling, then pour it onto the eggs, stirring all the time with a wooden spoon. Return the custard to the rinsed pan and heat gently, stirring continuously until the custard just coats the back of the spoon.

❹ Leave custard until cold—the mixture will cool quicker if transferred to a clean bowl—then chill thoroughly for at least one hour.

❺ Lightly whip the remaining cream until thick and floppy, then fold it into the chilled custard.

❻ Spoon or scrape the mixture into the ice-cream machine, and freeze-churn until ready to serve.

CHOCOLATE

An everyday family favourite.

INGREDIENTS

METHOD

4 large egg yolks

100 g/3¹/₂ oz caster sugar

2 Tbsp unsweetened cocoa powder

425 ml/15 fl oz milk

300 ml/10 fl oz single cream

Whisk the egg yolks and sugar together until thick and pale. Mix the cocoa to a smooth paste with a little of the milk, then heat the remaining milk until almost boiling. Pour the hot milk onto the cocoa paste and stir thoroughly, then return it to the pan, and bring it almost to the boil again.

Pour the cocoa onto the eggs, stirring continuously, then continue following the blueprint for Vanilla Ice Cream, from step 3 (see page 20). Freeze-churn until ready to serve.

CHILLI

Chillies and chocolate are both traditional Mexican foods, and they go together surprisingly well in ice cream, especially if you add some chopped fresh chillies for extra bite. Use dark, bitter chocolate if you prefer, but the white is very creamy and makes the chillies even more surprising! The quantity of sugar is much less for this recipe since white chocolate is so sweet.

INGREDIENTS

METHOD

300 ml/10 fl oz milk

1–2 small dried chillies

1 large cinnamon stick

4 large egg yolks

50 g/1³/₄ oz caster sugar

100 g/3¹/₂ oz white chocolate, finely chopped

300 ml/10 fl oz double cream

1 habanero chilli, very finely chopped (optional)

Heat the milk with the dried chillies and cinnamon until almost boiling. Remove from the heat, cover and leave for at least 20 minutes.

Whisk the egg yolks and sugar together until thick and pale. Remove the seasonings from the milk, then reheat it until almost boiling. Add the chopped chocolate to the milk, and stir until it has melted completely. Pour the chocolate milk onto the eggs, stirring all the time with a wooden spoon. Heat the mixture gently over a pan of hot (but not boiling water) for 3–4 minutes, until slightly thickened. Do not heat this mixture over direct heat or the chocolate may cause it to burn.

Continue as for the blueprint Extra-Rich Vanilla Ice Cream, from step 4 (see page 21), adding the lightly whipped cream to the chilled custard just before churning. Add the chopped habanero, if desired, to the ice cream just before churning is complete.

Chilli Ice Cream

CHOCOLATE FUDGE RIPPLE

It is not always easy to get a perfect ripple effect in home-made ice cream. I usually pack spoonfuls of the finished ice cream into a freezer tub, drizzling the sauce over as I go, to build up a chunky, abstract ripple which is then perfectly marbled when scooped from the container.

INGREDIENTS

4 large egg yolks

100 g/3¹/₂ oz caster sugar

300 ml/10 fl oz milk

¹/₂ tsp vanilla extract, or 1 tsp vanilla essence

300 ml/10 fl oz double cream

CHOCOLATE FUDGE SAUCE

100 g/3¹/₂ oz dark chocolate, broken into small pieces

3 Tbsp golden syrup

2 Tbsp hot water

1 tsp coffee essence (optional)

METHOD

Use the method from the blueprint for Vanilla Ice Cream (see page 20) to prepare a custard using the eggs, sugar and milk. Allow to cool completely, then add the vanilla and cream, and chill.

Prepare the chocolate fudge sauce while the custard is cooling. Using a small, heavy-based pan, melt the chocolate with the syrup, water and coffee essence, if used. Remove from the heat as soon as the chocolate has melted, then beat thoroughly. Allow to cool, then chill until required.

Freeze-churn the ice cream until ready to serve. Pack spoonfuls of the finished ice cream into a suitable freezer container, drizzling or spooning the sauce randomly over the scoops. Harden the ice cream in the freezer before serving, or store until required.

COFFEE CREAM PECAN

One of the most luxurious coffee ice creams I have tasted! The caramelized pecans add a sweet crunch.

INGREDIENTS

125 ml/4 fl oz hot (not boiling) water

40 g/4 Tbsp coarsely ground coffee

pinch of mixed spice

300 ml/10 fl oz single cream

4 large egg yolks

75 g/2³/₄ oz demerara sugar

100 g/3¹/₂ oz caster sugar

50 g/1³/₄ oz chopped pecan nuts

300 ml/10 fl oz double cream

METHOD

Pour the water over the coffee and leave to stand for at least five minutes. Strain the coffee into a pan with a pinch of mixed spice and the single cream, then heat gently until almost boiling. Meanwhile, whisk the egg yolks and demerara sugar together until pale and thick, then pour the coffee-flavoured cream onto the eggs, stirring continuously. Thicken and chill the custard, following the blueprint for Extra-Rich Vanilla, from step 4 (see page 21).

Prepare the caramelized nuts while the coffee custard is chilling. Melt the caster sugar slowly in a small, heavy pan, then bring to the boil and heat until golden brown. Add the chopped pecan nuts, shaking the caramel over them to coat them completely, then pour the mixture onto a lightly oiled baking sheet. Leave until completely cold and hard, then chop roughly.

Add the double cream to the coffee custard, and freeze-churn the mixture until thick. Add the chopped caramelized nuts, and continue churning until the ice cream is ready to serve.

Apple Cinnamon Ice Cream

*A*PPLE *C*INNAMON

A rich, fruity ice cream for the mellow months of the year. A crisp, tart apple gives the best flavour.

1 large or 2 small cinnamon sticks

300 ml/10 fl oz milk

4 large egg yolks

100 g/3¹/₂ oz caster sugar

¹/₂ tsp vanilla extract, or 1 tsp vanilla essence

300 ml/10 fl oz double cream

2 crisp tart eating apples, peeled and diced

1 tsp ground cinnamon

50 g/1³/₄ oz unsalted butter

METHOD

Heat the cinnamon sticks in the milk until almost boiling. Remove the pan from the heat, cover and leave for 20 minutes. Whisk the egg yolks and sugar together until thick and pale. Discard the cinnamon sticks, then reheat the milk, and continue making the custard following the blueprint for Vanilla Ice Cream, from step 2 (see page 20).

Prepare the cinnamon apples while the custard is cooling. Toss the chopped apples in the ground cinnamon. Heat the butter in a frying pan, and wait until the foam subsides, then add the apples with any remaining cinnamon and fry quickly until they just start to soften, stirring continuously. Allow to cool completely.

Freeze churn the ice cream until well thickened, then gradually add the cold apples while the ice-cream machine is still running, continuing churning until the ice cream is ready to serve.

*B*RANDIED *E*GGNOG

This ice cream has a subtle, sophisticated flavour, and can be used to accompany any number of pies,

cakes or other desserts.

INGREDIENTS

300 ml/10 fl oz single cream

1 vanilla pod

4 large egg yolks

100 g/3¹/₂ oz caster sugar

300 ml/10 fl oz double cream

4 Tbsp brandy

2 tsp freshly grated nutmeg (about 1 small nutmeg)

METHOD

Heat the single cream with the vanilla pod until almost boiling. Remove the pan from the heat, cover and leave for at least 20 minutes, or until cold. Remove the vanilla pod; rinse it well, and store for future use.

Continue following the blueprint for Extra-Rich Vanilla Ice Cream, from step 2 (see page 21), but add both the brandy and the nutmeg to the eggs and sugar before whisking them together.

Freeze-churn until ready to serve. The grated nutmeg gives an appealing, slightly flecked appearance to this ice cream.

*H*ONEY *&* *C*ARDAMOM

Cardamoms are most commonly used as a spice for Indian curries and other meat dishes, yet they are sweetly aromatic and make a wonderful flavouring for a number of breads, cakes and desserts, including ice cream.

INGREDIENTS

2 Tbsp green cardamom pods

300 ml/10 fl oz single cream

4 large egg yolks

1 Tbsp soft brown or light muscavado sugar

2 heaped Tbsp honey

300 ml/10 fl oz double cream

METHOD

Crush the cardamoms in a mortar and pestle, or with the end of a rolling pin, until they have all split and the seeds have fallen out. Pick out and discard the husks, rubbing them with your fingers to remove any remaining seeds. Heat the seeds with the single cream until almost boiling. Remove from the heat, then cover and leave for at least 20 minutes.

Continue, following the blueprint for Extra-Rich Vanilla Ice Cream, from step 2 (see page 21). You may like to strain the cardamom seeds out of the cream before completing the custard, but I prefer to leave them in.

Fold the honey into the chilled custard with the double cream, then freeze-churn until ready to serve.

*G*INGER

Ginger is a hot flavouring, which, like chillies, makes a perfect ice cream. In this recipe the cream has a mild flavour, spiced up by the pieces of chopped ginger folded in at the end of churning.

INGREDIENTS

100 g/3^1/$_2$ oz fresh root ginger, grated

4 large egg yolks

75 g/2^3/$_4$ oz soft brown or light muscavado sugar

juice of half a lemon

300 ml/10 fl oz single cream

300 ml/10 fl oz double cream

100 g/3^1/$_2$ oz preserved or glacé ginger, finely chopped

METHOD

Grate the ginger coarsely; do not peel it, just grate the whole lot, skin as well. Beat the egg yolks and sugar together until thick and pale. Firmly squeeze the ginger in your hand, or with the back of a ladle through a fine sieve, to extract all the juice, adding it to the egg yolks with the lemon juice. Heat the single cream until almost boiling, then pour it onto the gingered egg mixture, stirring all the time.

Finish the ice cream following the blueprint recipe for Extra-Rich Vanilla Ice Cream, from step 3 (see page 21). Add the chopped ginger to the mixture in the ice-cream machine just before churning is complete and the ice cream is ready to serve.

BROWN BREAD

This ice cream is based on an English Victorian recipe, and, despite sounding somewhat frugal, is nutty, creamy and delicious. The secret is to toast the breadcrumbs until they are dry and crispy; do not use them soft, or the finished ice cream will be soggy in texture.

INGREDIENTS

4 large egg yolks

100 g/3½ oz caster sugar

425 ml/15 fl oz milk

½ tsp vanilla extract, or 1 tsp vanilla essence

50 g/1¾ oz fresh wholemeal breadcrumbs

300 ml/10 fl oz double cream

METHOD

Use the eggs, sugar, milk and vanilla to make a custard, following the blueprint for Vanilla Ice Cream (see page 20). Allow to cool, then chill for at least an hour.

Meanwhile, toast the breadcrumbs in the oven or under the grill until well browned and completely dry, tossing them over several times. Allow to cool completely. The crumbs should be very crisp, or they will become a soggy goo in the ice cream.

Whip the cream until soft and floppy, then fold it into the chilled custard along with the breadcrumbs. Freeze-churn until ready to serve.

$\mathcal{P}$ISTACHIO

Pistachio ice cream is usually made in the Italian style, and I adore these flavoursome nuts.

Adding a little mascarpone cheese is not essential, but is deliciously decadent!

INGREDIENTS

4 large egg yolks

100 g/3^1/$_2$ oz caster sugar

425 ml/15 fl oz milk

^{1}/$_2$ tsp vanilla extract, or 1 tsp vanilla essence

2 Tbsp mascarpone cheese (optional)

3 Tbsp Amaretto or other nut liqueur or

100 ml/3^1/$_2$ fl oz sweet Italian dessert wine (optional)

300 ml/10 fl oz double cream

75 g/2^3/$_4$ oz pistachios, shelled

METHOD

Use the eggs, sugar and milk to make a custard, following the method in the blueprint for Vanilla Ice Cream (see page 20). Beat together the vanilla flavouring, mascarpone and liqueur or dessert wine, then pour the hot, thickened custard (completed to the end of step 3) onto the mixture and blend well. Allow to cool completely, then chill for at least an hour.

Whip the cream until thick and floppy, then fold it into the chilled custard. Freeze-churn until thick, then add the pistachios and continue churning until the ice cream is ready to serve.

$\mathcal{D}$OUBLE $\mathcal{C}$HOC $\mathcal{C}$HIP

For chocoholics everywhere! Use the best chocolate you can (70 per cent cocoa solids is ideal),

since both flavour and texture are so much better.

INGREDIENTS

1 large or 2 small cinnamon sticks

300 ml/10 fl oz single cream

4 large egg yolks

75 g/2^3/$_4$ oz soft brown or light muscavado sugar

125 g/4^1/$_2$ oz chocolate, finely chopped

300 ml/10 fl oz double cream

50 g/1^3/$_4$ oz chocolate, roughly chopped

METHOD

Heat the cinnamon sticks with the single cream until almost boiling, then cover the pan and leave them to infuse for 20 minutes. Remove the sticks.

Whisk together the egg yolks and sugar until thick and slightly paler in colour. Reheat the cream until almost boiling, then add in the finely chopped chocolate and stir until it has melted completely. Pour the mixture onto the eggs, stirring continuously, then heat gently over a pan of hot (but not boiling) water for 3–4 minutes, until slightly thickened. Do not heat this mixture in a saucepan over direct heat since the chocolate may cause it to burn.

Cool the custard, and then chill it lightly for 30–40 minutes; it will become very thick. Lightly whip the double cream, fold it into the chilled custard and then freeze-churn the mixture. Add the chocolate chips once the cream has thickened in the ice-cream machine, then continue churning until it is ready to serve.

Pistachio Ice Cream

CHOCOLATE COOKIE

This is a very quick way to make something really special. Use your favourite confectionery bar: chocolate-covered toffee or caramel work well, but my favourite is a crisp, chocolate-covered wafer.

4 large egg yolks

75 g/2³/₄ oz caster sugar

300 ml/10 fl oz milk

1 tsp vanilla extract, or 2 tsp vanilla essence

300 ml/10 fl oz double cream

2 x 48 g/2 oz chocolate wafer bars of your choice, roughly chopped

METHOD

Make a basic ice-cream mixture following the blueprint for Vanilla Ice Cream (see page 20). Freeze-churn the mixture until almost ready to serve, then add the chopped wafers. Continue churning until ready to serve.

ENGLISH TOFFEE

Sweet, buttery and irresistible—a combination of the best vanilla ice cream and favourite buttery sweet.

INGREDIENTS

300 ml/10 fl oz single cream

1 vanilla pod

4 large egg yolks

100 g/3¹/₂ oz caster sugar

300 ml/10 fl oz double cream

BUTTERSCOTCH SAUCE

2 Tbsp butter

2 Tbsp demerara sugar

1 Tbsp golden syrup

50 ml/2 fl oz milk

125 g/4¹/₂ oz soft English toffees, chopped

METHOD

Prepare and chill the ice cream, following the blueprint for Extra-Rich Vanilla Ice Cream (see page 21).

While the custard for the ice cream is cooling (step 4), make the Butterscotch Sauce. Heat the butter, sugar and syrup together in a small, heavy-based pan until the butter has melted and the ingredients have blended together. Boil rapidly until the mixture is at 115°C/235°F, or soft ball stage (this should be marked on your sugar thermometer). Cool the mixture slightly, then gradually beat in the milk. Allow to cool completely, then chill until required.

Freeze-churn the ice cream until thickened, then add the chopped toffees with the motor still running, or fold them into the ice cream with a spoon. Continue churning until the ice cream is ready to serve.

Pack spoonfuls of the finished ice cream into a suitable freezer container, drizzling or spooning the sauce randomly over the scoops. Harden the ice cream in the freezer for 15–20 minutes before serving, or store until required.

NEW ORLEANS PRALINE

Heavy with rum and caramelized pecans, this is a vanilla ice cream with a potent crunch!

INGREDIENTS

300 ml/10 fl oz single cream

1 vanilla pod

4 large egg yolks

100 g/3¹/₂ oz caster sugar

300 ml/10 fl oz double cream

3 Tbsp rum

CARAMELIZED PECANS:

50 g/1³/₄ oz caster sugar

50 g/1³/₄ oz pecan nuts, roughly chopped

METHOD

Make up a batch of Extra-Rich Vanilla Ice Cream, following the blueprint (see page 21), but add the rum to the thickened custard just before cooling (at the end of step 3).

Prepare the nuts while the custard is cooling. Melt the sugar slowly in a small, heavy pan, then bring to the boil and heat until golden brown. Add in the chopped pecan nuts, shaking the caramel over them to coat them completely. Pour the mixture onto a lightly oiled baking sheet. Leave until completely hard and cold, then chop roughly.

Freeze-churn, adding the chopped nuts just before churning is complete.

MOCHA ALMOND

This is a sophisticated ice cream to be enjoyed on its own. Serve in tall, elegant glasses with crisp, light biscuits or wafers.

INGREDIENTS

125 ml/4 fl oz hot (not boiling) water

40 g/4 Tbsp coarsely ground coffee

300 ml/10 fl oz single cream

pinch of mixed spice

4 large egg yolks

75 g/2³/₄ oz demerara sugar

300 ml/10 fl oz double cream

CHOCOLATE FUDGE SAUCE

100 g/3¹/₂ oz good dark chocolate, broken into small pieces

3 Tbsp golden syrup

2 Tbsp hot water

1 tsp coffee essence (optional)

50 g/1³/₄ oz toasted almonds, roughly chopped

METHOD

Pour the water over the coffee and leave to stand for at least five minutes. Strain the coffee into a pan with the single cream and a pinch of mixed spice, then heat gently until almost boiling. Meanwhile, whisk the egg yolks and demerara sugar together until pale and thick, then pour the coffee-flavoured cream onto the eggs, stirring continuously. Continue as for the Extra-Rich Vanilla Ice Cream blueprint, from step 3 (see page 21).

Prepare the Chocolate Fudge Sauce while the custard is chilling. Place all the ingredients in a small, heavy-based pan, and heat gently until the chocolate has melted and they have blended together. Beat thoroughly, then allow to cool before chilling.

Freeze-churn the ice cream until ready to serve, adding the chopped almonds towards the end of the churning process. Spoon the chocolate sauce over the ice cream as it is scooped into a freezer container, then harden in the freezer for at least 30 minutes before serving.

MINT CHOCOLATE CHIP

As I said before, I see no point in making ice cream at home unless you can improve on the

excellent commercial products now available. One flavouring that I hate is very thin, synthetic mint.

Crème de menthe is far more luxurious and yummy.

INGREDIENTS

300 ml/10 fl oz single cream

1 vanilla pod

4 large egg yolks

100 g/3½ oz caster sugar

300 ml/10 fl oz double cream

3 Tbsp crème de menthe

50 g/1¾ oz chocolate chips or roughly chopped chocolate, or a little more if you like

METHOD

Make up a batch of Extra-Rich Vanilla Ice Cream, following the blueprint (see page 21), but add the crème de menthe to the thickened custard just before cooling (at the end of step 3).

Freeze-churn the ice cream until almost ready to serve, then add the chocolate chips and finish churning.

CHOCOLATE COOKIE DOUGH

Serious addiction swiftly follows the first mouthful of this ice cream. If you don't want to get hooked,

turn the page now!

INGREDIENTS

300 ml/10 fl oz single cream

1 vanilla pod

4 large egg yolks

100 g/3½ oz caster sugar

300 ml/10 fl oz double cream

COOKIE DOUGH

125 g/4½ oz plain flour

1 Tbsp unsweetened cocoa powder, sieved

75 g/2¾ oz butter

75 g/2¾ oz caster sugar

50 g/1¾ oz roughly chopped chocolate chips

water to mix, if necessary

METHOD

Make up a quantity of Extra-Rich Vanilla Ice Cream following the method in the blueprint (see page 21).

Prepare the cookie dough while the custard for the ice cream is cooling. Blend together the flour, cocoa and butter. Stir in the sugar and chocolate chips, then bring the mixture together into a firm dough, adding a few drops of water to mix if necessary. Knead the dough thoroughly, then cover with cling film and chill. (You will need about half the dough for the ice cream, but it is difficult to make a smaller quantity. Add more if you wish, or freeze the remainder for later use—you could bake it up into cookies!) Chop the dough roughly before you add it to the ice cream.

Freeze-churn the ice cream until thick, then fold in as much chopped dough as your conscience will allow. Continue churning, or harden in the freezer before serving.

STRAWBERRY

Use freshly picked, ripe fruit to get the best possible strawberry flavour.

This is light, creamy and non-custard based. It is utterly delicious.

INGREDIENTS

450 g/1 lb strawberries, hulled

juice of half a lemon, or to taste

150–200 g/5$^{1}/_{2}$–7 oz sieved icing sugar, to taste

300 ml/10 fl oz double cream

VARIATIONS

1–2 Tbsp freshly chopped mint OR

1–2 tsp freshly ground black pepper

METHOD

❶ Purée the strawberries in a blender or food processor, then turn them into a bowl and season with the lemon juice and sugar to taste. Add the mint or black pepper, if used.

❷ Stir in the cream.

❸ Freeze-churn until the ice cream is ready to serve.

BLACKBERRY

The flavour of blackberries is unlike that of any other fruit, full of strong, mellow sweetness. Of course, they have to be fully ripened to taste this way, which means getting to them before the birds, if you are picking your own. If no blackberry liqueur is to hand, use a sweet vermouth or port.

INGREDIENTS

450 g/1 lb blackberries

juice of 1 lemon

150 g/5$^{1}/_{2}$ oz sieved icing sugar, or to taste

3 Tbsp blackberry liqueur (optional)

300 ml/10 fl oz double cream

METHOD

Blend the blackberries with the lemon juice, then stir in the sugar until dissolved. Sieve the fruit to remove any seeds. Add the blackberry liqueur.

Continue following the blueprint for Strawberry Ice Cream, from step 2 (see above), then freeze-churn until ready to serve.

Strawberry Ice Cream

PUMPKIN PIE

This is inspired by the traditional American Thanksgiving dessert. You do not have to add the raisins, but I think they lend an extra sweetness to what might otherwise be a slightly spicy ice cream.

INGREDIENTS

225 g/8 oz thick pumpkin purée, fresh or canned

100 g/3¹/₂ oz icing sugar, sieved

1 tsp ground cinnamon

1 tsp ground ginger

1 tsp ground nutmeg

juice of half a lemon

250 ml/9 fl oz evaporated milk

300 ml/10 fl oz double cream

75 g/2³/₄ oz raisins or sultanas

METHOD

Beat the pumpkin with the sugar, spices, lemon juice and evaporated milk. Beat the cream until thickened and slightly floppy, then fold it into the pumpkin mixture. Chill for one hour, or continue immediately if all the ingredients are cold.

Freeze-churn until ready to serve, adding the fruit to the ice cream just before churning is complete.

LEMON & LIME

This recipe is so simple and so delicious! The fresh, tangy flavour seems to go with just about any dessert, but I like to eat this ice cream just as it is—it's probably my favourite summer ice cream.

INGREDIENTS

200 g/7 oz caster sugar

200 ml/8 fl oz water

2 large lemons, grated rind and juice

2 limes, grated rind and juice

300 ml/10 fl oz double cream (or a mixture of double and single)

METHOD

Dissolve the sugar in the water with the grated rinds, then simmer slowly for 20 minutes to give a very light syrup. Allow to cool completely, then add the fruit juices and strain through a sieve to remove the rinds and any pips.

Lightly whip the cream until thick and floppy, then gradually whisk in the fruit syrup. Pour the mixture into the ice-cream machine, and freeze-churn until ready to serve.

Pumpkin Pie Ice Cream

ENGLISH PLUM & CINNAMON

This is an unusual, fruity ice cream full of old-fashioned flavours.

I sometimes use damsons in place of plums, which gives a sharper flavour. Serve with shortbread fingers,

brandy snaps or a luxurious compôte of autumn fruits.

INGREDIENTS

450 g/1 lb dessert plums, stones removed

100 g/3½ oz caster sugar

1 large or 2 small cinnamon sticks

50 ml/2 fl oz water

juice of half a lemon, or to taste

425 ml/15 fl oz double cream

METHOD

Slowly cook the plums with the sugar, cinnamon and water in a covered pan until the fruits burst and start to become pulpy. Allow to cool, ensuring that the cinnamon sticks are still buried in the fruit for maximum flavour.

Remove the cinnamon once the fruit has cooled, add lemon juice to taste, then purée the plums in a blender or food processor. Rub the purée through a sieve, add a little more sugar if necessary, then chill for at least an hour.

Measure the purée: you should have about 425 ml/15 fl oz, so make it up with a little water, if necessary. Add the cream, then freeze-churn until ready to serve.

CARAMEL

A sophisticated ice cream by itself, or a brilliantly complementary accompaniment to apple or plum pie. I like to serve the ice cream in tall glasses, spiked with extravagantly huge shards of caramel. The flavour is subtle, so do not serve this after a highly spiced main course.

INGREDIENTS

100 g/3½ oz caster sugar

600 ml/1 pint single cream

3 large egg yolks

150 ml/5 fl oz double cream, beaten until thick and floppy

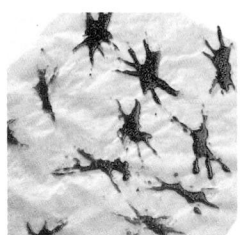

METHOD

Heat the sugar very slowly in a pan until dissolved, then increase the heat and bring the syrup to the boil. Continue cooking, without stirring, until it turns a rich chestnut brown.

Meanwhile, heat the single cream gently until almost boiling, then take it off the heat and beat the hot caramel into it. This is a critical operation! If the cream is not hot enough, the caramel will spit and form into balls in the mixture. If the cream is left on the heat while the caramel is added it might boil, which is not a great idea. Don't be put off, however—just keep a close eye on both pans! Allow the caramel cream to cool completely.

Stir the beaten egg yolks into the chilled mixture with the double cream, then freeze-churn until ready to serve.

SORBETS

blueprint sorbet PAPAYA LIME

LEMON-LIME

GUNPOWDER

STRAWBERRY & KIWI FRUIT

TANGY CRANBERRY

APRICOT, ORANGE & LEMON

SAFFRON KIR ROYALE

MANGO & GINGER

MARGARITA

MOCHA

CINNAMON APPLE

HONEYDEW MELON

ORANGE TEQUILA

GAZPACHO

*S*orbets are lighter and more refreshing than ice creams, and are usually made with fruit, either juice or a purée. They are sharper in flavour and much lower in calories than ice creams since they do not contain cream or egg yolks, though they sometimes include egg whites.

Sorbets are traditionally based on a sugar syrup. Most are made with ripe fruits that do not require cooking, since these have freshness of flavour not generally found in other varieties.

Sorbets that are made with fruit juice tend to make a greater bulk than those based on fruit purées. I have adapted my recipes so that they should not overflow the standard ice-cream machine, but take care if you are a juicer fanatic and start experimenting with your own recipes!

These sorbets are traditionally served either as a dessert or to cleanse the palate. Those with egg white tend to be a little less icy than those without, and all are best served freshly churned. I usually prefer to serve sorbet straight from the ice-cream machine, but if they are hardened in the freezer they need very little tempering; 10 minutes is usually ample, or 15 minutes in the fridge. Sorbets stored for any length of time may become crumbly in the freezer. This can easily be rectified, however, by whizzing the mixture in a food processor just before serving.

Traditionalists would call a sorbet that includes alcohol a punch. Wines make very good sorbets, and liqueurs can be used to emphasize the flavour of fruits. Alcohol tends to slow the rate of freezing, so extra churning time may be needed. Most sorbets take about 15 minutes to churn, those with alcohol a little longer.

Not all sorbets are fruit based: green tea makes a refreshing summer sorbet, just as a glass of iced tea is welcome on a very hot day. Some of the alcoholic sorbets in this chapter make wonderful summer aperitifs.

PAPAYA LIME

Two excitingly flavoured fruits combine to make a really tropical sorbet. Use ripe papayas, which should have a yellowy-green skin. Keep the seeds from the papaya to decorate the sorbet; these are edible, but, be warned: they are surprisingly peppery. I sometimes serve this sorbet in spoonfuls in thin almond tuilles, or biscuits.

INGREDIENTS

175 g/6 oz caster sugar

425 ml/15 fl oz water

1 lime, grated rind and juice

2 ripe papayas or pawpaws

METHOD

❶ Dissolve the sugar slowly in the water, then bring to the boil. Add the lime rind, then simmer the syrup for five minutes. Remove the pan from the heat and leave until completely cool.

❷ Peel and roughly chop the papayas, reserving the black seeds for garnish. Add the lime juice, then blend until smooth in a blender or food processor.

❸ Strain the cooled sugar syrup through a sieve to remove the rind. Combine the syrup with the papaya purée, mix thoroughly, then spoon into the ice-cream machine. Freeze-churn until ready to serve.

ℓEMON-LIME

Tangy citrus juices give this sorbet a clean, bright, refreshing flavour, which cuts through and balances the richness of many desserts. I love to serve this with traditional mince pies at Christmas.

INGREDIENTS

3 lemons, grated rind and juice

2 limes, grated rind and juice

water

175 g/6 oz caster sugar

1 large egg white

METHOD

Mix together the lemon and lime juices, then make them up to 425 ml/ 15 fl oz with the addition of cold water. Add the sugar, then continue as for the blueprint for Papaya Lime Sorbet (opposite), but do not add the grated rinds yet. Follow the blueprint recipe to the end of step 1.

Lightly beat the egg white with a fork, then add the cooled syrup and the grated rinds. Pour into the ice-cream machine and freeze-churn until ready to serve.

GUNPOWDER

Not as explosive as it sounds! This delicate sorbet may be made with any green tea; use your favourite.

Gunpowder tea is in tight balls when dry, which burst into very large leaves once hot water is added.

INGREDIENTS

300 ml/10 fl oz boiling water

8 Tbsp gunpowder tea, or other large-leaf green tea

150 g/5¹/₂ oz caster sugar

600 ml/1 pint cold water

1 lemon, grated rind and juice

1 large egg white

METHOD

Pour boiling water over the tea and leave to infuse for 10 minutes. Heat the sugar slowly with the cold water until dissolved. Bring to the boil, then simmer for five minutes. Mix the tea with the syrup, lemon rind and juice, then allow it to cool completely. Strain the mixture when completely cold.

Lightly beat the egg white with a fork, then add it to the cold tea mixture before pouring into the ice-cream machine. Freeze-churn until ready to serve.

STRAWBERRY & KIWI FRUIT

This sorbet has a stunning colour, enhanced by the flecks of seeds from the kiwi fruits. A perfect

accompaniment to strawberry tartlets or shortbreads.

INGREDIENTS

225 g/8 oz caster sugar

300 ml/10 fl oz water

350 g/12 oz strawberries, hulled and roughly chopped

3 kiwi fruits, peeled and chopped

juice of 2 lemons

2 tsp freshly ground black pepper

METHOD

Prepare the sugar syrup as in the blueprint for Papaya Lime Sorbet (see page 44), but do not add any citrus rind. Allow to cool completely.

Blend the strawberries to a smooth purée along with the kiwi fruits and lemon juice, then add the cold sugar syrup and black pepper. Pour the mixture into the ice-cream machine, and freeze-churn until ready to serve.

Strawberry & Kiwi Fruit Sorbet

Tangy Cranberry Sorbet

TANGY CRANBERRY

I leave the berries very finely chopped in this sorbet, though you may prefer to sieve it.

Sweeten the mixture more, if you wish, but cranberries should be quite sharp and very refreshing.

Serve with thin, orange-flavoured biscuits.

INGREDIENTS

300 g/10½ oz cranberries

175 g/6 oz caster sugar

2 oranges, grated rind and juice

250 ml/9 fl oz water

2 large cinnamon sticks

METHOD

Heat all the ingredients together gently until the berries burst, about 10–15 minutes. Allow the fruits to cool, then remove the cinnamon sticks and blend until almost smooth in a blender or food processor.

Turn the mixture into the ice-cream machine, then freeze-churn until ready to serve.

APRICOT, ORANGE, & LEMON

Dried apricots have so much texture they even make a substantial sorbet! This is a good iced dessert to make in

the winter, when fresh soft fruits are out of season. Serve with any fruit compôtes, pies or crumbles.

INGREDIENTS

125 g/4½ oz caster sugar

425 ml/15 fl oz water

1 tsp crushed cardamom seeds (optional)

175 g/6 oz ready-to-eat dried apricots

1 orange, grated rind and juice

250 ml/9 fl oz orange juice

1 lemon, grated rind and juice

METHOD

Prepare the sugar syrup as for the Papaya Lime blueprint (see page 44), adding the cardamom seeds, if desired. Leave to cool completely.

Soak the apricots with the orange rind and juice, plus the extra orange juice, for 30 minutes. Whizz the apricot and orange mixture in a liquidizer or food processor until smooth. Mix the purée with the cold sugar syrup and the lemon rind and juice, then pour into the ice-cream machine. Freeze-churn until ready to serve.

SAFFRON KIR ROYALE

This must be the ultimate answer to sophisticated summer entertaining: an iced aperitif.

Don't worry if it sounds a funny mix of ingredients—it works perfectly.

INGREDIENTS

125 g/4¹/₂ oz caster sugar

large pinch of saffron strands

350 ml/12 fl oz water

750 ml/28 fl oz champagne or dry sparkling wine

crème de cassis for serving

METHOD

Use the sugar, saffron and water to make a sugar syrup following the method in the Papaya Lime blueprint (see page 44). Sieve the cold syrup to remove any remaining saffron strands, if necessary.

Mix the cooled syrup with the champagne, then turn into the ice-cream machine. Freeze-churn until ready to serve.

Scoop into chilled champagne flutes and drizzle a little crème de cassis over the sorbet before serving.

MANGO & GINGER

A little ginger can really enhance the flavor of mangoes that have been artificially ripened in transit, rather than being coaxed into peak condition in the sunshine while attached to a tree!

INGREDIENTS

175 g/6 oz caster sugar

450 ml/16 fl oz water

1¹/₂ tsp ground ginger

1 large, ripe mango

juice of 1 lemon

METHOD

Prepare a sugar syrup from the sugar, water and ground ginger, following the method in the blueprint sorbet, step 1 (see page 44).

Peel the mango and cut the flesh away from the stone. Process the mango in a liquidizer or food processor with the lemon juice until smooth, then add the cold sugar syrup and mix well.

Turn the mixture into the machine, and freeze-churn until ready to serve.

M ARGARITA

Another alcohol-based sorbet to serve as an aperitif. Sprinkling salt over the sorbet will encourage it to melt,

so harden the mixture in the freezer for 15–20 minutes before serving, if necessary.

INGREDIENTS

200 g/7 oz caster sugar

500 ml/18 fl oz water

3 limes, grated rind and juice

125 ml/4 fl oz tequila

50 ml/2 fl oz Triple Sec

coarse salt and fresh lime to serve

METHOD

Use the sugar and water to make a sugar syrup, following the method in the blueprint for Papaya Lime Sorbet, step 1 (see page 44).

Add the rind and juice of the limes to the cold syrup with the tequila and Triple Sec. Stir well, then pour into the ice-cream machine. Freeze-churn until hard enough to scoop into chilled glasses, or harden the mixture in the freezer for 15–20 minutes if necessary.

Serve in chilled glasses, decorated with a slice or a wedge of lime, and sprinkled with coarse salt.

M OCHA

This sorbet makes a refreshing end to a meal on a balmy night, in place of hot coffee and chocolates. Try

serving it in Irish coffee glasses with a splash of whisky and a dollop of lightly whipped cream.

INGREDIENTS

250 ml/9 fl oz almost boiling water

50 g/1³/₄ oz coarsely ground coffee, as strong a blend as possible

2 Tbsp unsweetened cocoa powder

1 lemon, grated rind and juice

100 g/3¹/₂ oz soft brown sugar

450 ml/16 fl oz water

METHOD

Pour the almost boiling water onto the coffee and cocoa powder. Stir well, then remove from the heat and stir in the lemon rind and juice. Leave for 15–20 minutes to infuse, then strain through a sieve and leave until completely cold.

Prepare the sugar syrup from the brown sugar and remaining water while the coffee is infusing. Follow the blueprint method for Papaya Lime Sorbet, step 1 (see page 44).

Combine the sugar syrup with the mocha infusion, then pour into the ice-cream machine. Freeze-churn until ready to serve.

Margarita Sorbet

Honeydew Melon Sorbet

CINNAMON APPLE

This unusual sharp and fruity sorbet is perfect for serving with caramelized apple slices

and a caramel sauce, or French Apple Tart.

INGREDIENTS

2 medium cooking apples, peeled, cored, and sliced

125 ml/4 fl oz water

425 ml/15 fl oz apple juice

50 g/1³/₄ oz caster sugar

2 large cinnamon sticks

4 cloves

1 lemon, grated rind and juice

1 Tbsp Calvados (optional)

METHOD

Cook the apples over a medium heat for 15 minutes, along with the water, apple juice, sugar, spices and lemon rind. Stir from time to time to prevent the apples from sticking. Remove the pan from the heat and allow to cool completely.

Remove the spices from the cooked apple, then whizz in a liquidizer or food processor until smooth. Add the lemon juice and Calvados, and any extra sugar required to give a fairly sweet purée. Scrape the mixture into the ice-cream machine, and freeze-churn until ready to serve.

HONEYDEW MELON

If you think of melon as a watery nothingness, think again. In this recipe, I have used crème de menthe to

bring out the flavour of the melon; you could also try Midori, the melon liqueur. I like to serve this with balls

of watermelon, to provide an exciting colour contrast, and the crisp biscuits known as langue du chat.

INGREDIENTS

125 g/4¹/₂ oz caster sugar

350 ml/12 fl oz water

1 Tbsp lemon juice

1 small honeydew melon (about 675 g/1¹/₂ lb)

1 large egg white

1–1¹/₂ Tbsp crème de menthe

mint leaves to decorate

METHOD

Prepare a sugar syrup from the sugar and water following the method for the blueprint sorbet step 1 (see page 44). Add the lemon juice after boiling, then leave until completely cold.

Blend the melon to a smooth purée in a liquidizer or food processor, then blend in the cooled sugar syrup. Whisk the egg white until soft and frothy, then fold in the melon mixture with crème de menthe to taste.

Turn into the ice-cream machine, then freeze-churn until ready to serve. Decorate with mint leaves.

ORANGE TEQUILA

This makes a lovely dessert after a spicy Mexican meal of tacos or fajitas. Serve as a topping to

a fruit salad of ripe tropical fruits, such as melon, papaya, mango and strawberries.

INGREDIENTS

METHOD

2 large oranges, grated rind and juice

125 g/4½ oz caster sugar

orange juice

125 ml/4 fl oz tequila

Use very finely grated orange rind for this recipe. Mix the rind with the sugar, then add the juice, making it up to 425 ml/15 fl oz with extra orange juice or water. Stir in the tequila, and continue stirring until the sugar has dissolved.

1 large egg white

Lightly whisk the egg white until frothy, then whisk in the orange mixture.

GAZPACHO

This piquant sorbet makes an unusual starter, excellent to serve while waiting for your drumsticks to cook on

the barbecue. Serve in glasses, garnished with finely diced salad vegetables such as

peppers, cucumber and spring onions. The flavour will become much stronger if frozen;

I prefer to serve it straight from the ice-cream machine.

INGREDIENTS

METHOD

1 Tbsp caster sugar

125 ml/4 fl oz water

425 ml/15 fl oz tomato juice

1–2 Tbsp tomato purée

2 spring onions, trimmed and chopped

½ green pepper, seeds removed and chopped

1 green chilli, seeds removed and chopped

1 small clove garlic

1 Tbsp lemon juice

dash of Worcestershire sauce

salt and freshly ground black pepper

Use the sugar and water to make a sugar syrup, following the method for the blueprint Papaya Lime Sorbet step 1 (see page 44). Allow to cool completely.

Blend all the remaining ingredients together into a smooth purée in a liquidizer or food processor. Press the purée through a sieve, using the back of a ladle to force it through; this will give a very smooth base for the sorbet.

Combine the sugar syrup with the sieved tomato mixture, season well, then pour into the ice-cream machine. Freeze-churn until ready to serve.

Gazpacho Sorbet

S H E R B E T S

blueprint sherbet REAL PINEAPPLE

ORANGE CHOCOLATE CHIP

TANGERINE

PINEAPPLE BUTTERMILK

PINA COLADA

TROPICAL

CAPPUCCINO

MANGO

PINK LEMONADE

RASPBERRY

WATERMELON

A sherbet is very similar to a sorbet, but uses a proportion of milk to make the mixture slightly more creamy. Home-made sherbets can be made positively luxurious by adding single or even double cream to the mixture. I sometimes add buttermilk, which gives more richness than ordinary milk, but also adds a touch of piquancy. It works well, but you should ensure that the main flavouring of the sherbet will not be masked by the buttermilk—an acid fruit such as rhubarb is perfect.

Sherbets sometimes contain egg whites, which are whipped until frothy before being incorporated into the mixture. The main rule for successful sherbet-making is to mix the syrup, fruit and egg whites (if used) together just before freeze-churning. As many mixtures contain lemon juice as a seasoning, combining the ingredients any sooner may result in a curdling of the dairy products. If your mixture should curdle, a quick whizz in the food processor should blend the ingredients together again.

Sherbets are really my idea of a perfect ice dessert. They are not too rich and filling, they work particularly well with fruits and are therefore refreshing, and they are relatively quick to make. Most take about 20 minutes to freeze-churn, and they can be served straight from the ice-cream machine. They can be hardened for a little while before serving, if you prefer, but prolonged freezer storage tends to make them crumbly.

Sherbets need very little tempering before serving if they have been frozen; 10 minutes at room temperature or 20 minutes in the fridge is usually sufficient. If you wish to serve a selection of ice desserts, try a scoop of sherbet with one of ice cream for a good contrast in texture and creaminess.

REAL PINEAPPLE

All pineapple sherbets are clean and fresh in flavour.

You will need about a quarter of a large fruit to make this recipe.

INGREDIENTS

175 g/6 oz caster sugar

200 ml/7 fl oz water

2 large egg whites

150 g/5½ oz fresh pineapple purée

1 Tbsp lemon juice

125 ml/4 fl oz double cream

METHOD

❶ Heat the sugar slowly in the water until dissolved, then bring to the boil and simmer for 15 minutes. Remove the pan from the heat, and allow the syrup to cool completely.

❷ Beat the egg whites in a large bowl until white and foamy. Combine them with the pineapple purée and lemon juice, stir well, then add the cold syrup.

❸ Stir in the cream just before pouring the mixture into the ice-cream machine. Freeze-churn until ready to serve.

ORANGE CHOCOLATE CHIP

A light, creamy sherbet with a tang of orange and the luxury of chocolate. Try serving with a sauce made

with tangy orange marmalade, thinned down with water or orange juice.

INGREDIENTS

150 ml/5 fl oz water

175 g/6 oz caster sugar

1 orange, grated rind and juice

orange juice (about 250 ml/9 fl oz)

1 Tbsp lemon juice

3 large egg whites

125 ml/4 fl oz double cream

40 g/1½ oz roughly cut chocolate chips

METHOD

Prepare a syrup from the water, sugar and orange rind, following the method in the blueprint sherbet, step 1 (above). Cool completely.

Squeeze the juice from the orange, measure it, and make it up to 350 ml/ 12 fl oz with orange juice. Add the lemon juice.

Continue as for the blueprint recipe, step 2, adding first the fruit juices, then the sugar syrup, and then the cream to the egg whites.

Add the chocolate chips to the sherbet about halfway through churning, then continue until the sherbet is ready to serve.

Orange Chocolate Chip Sherbet

TANGERINE

The elegant sweetness of tangerines flavours this simple, refreshing sherbet. Clementines may also be used,

but try to avoid fruits with pips, which need more preparation before blending.

600 ml/1 pint milk

125 g/4¹/₂ oz caster sugar

250 ml/9 fl oz sieved tangerine purée (about 4

medium fruits)

juice of half a lemon

METHOD

Prepare a syrup from the milk and sugar, following the blueprint method for Real Pineapple Sherbet, step 1 (see page 60). Allow to cool completely.

Purée the tangerines in a food processor, then rub the mixture through a sieve. Stir in the lemon juice just before adding the fruits to the sugar syrup.

Freeze-churn until ready to serve.

PINEAPPLE BUTTERMILK

Buttermilk adds a tangy freshness to this pineapple sherbet.

You will need about half a medium fruit to make the purée.

INGREDIENTS

225 g/8 oz fresh pineapple purée

175 g/6 oz caster sugar

juice of 1 lemon

425 ml/15 fl oz buttermilk

METHOD

Mix together the pineapple, sugar and lemon juice, and leave to stand for at least one hour. Stir from time to time to ensure the sugar has dissolved.

Gradually whisk the buttermilk into the pineapple, then pour into the ice-cream machine. Freeze-churn until ready to serve.

PINA COLADA

I have used coconut milk, the creamed flesh of the coconut, for this sherbet. Use creamed coconut dissolved in milk if coconut milk is not available, but many supermarkets now stock it as it is an essential ingredient in Thai cookery.

INGREDIENTS

200 g/7 oz coconut milk

350 ml/12 fl oz milk

100 g/3½ oz caster sugar

250 ml/9 fl oz pineapple juice

4 Tbsp Malibu or white rum

fresh pineapple and cherries to decorate

METHOD

Stir the coconut milk, milk and sugar together until the sugar has dissolved, then add the remaining ingredients.

Turn the mixture immediately into the ice-cream machine. Freeze-churn until ready to serve. Serve decorated with cherries and fresh pineapple.

TROPICAL

A luxurious mixture of mango, kiwi fruit and fresh pineapple makes an exotic,

tropical sherbet that is very refreshing.

METHOD

600 ml/1 pint milk

125 g/4¹/₂ oz caster sugar

half a mango

1 kiwi fruit

3 Tbsp pineapple purée or crushed pineapple

juice of 1 lime

Prepare a syrup from the milk and sugar, following the blueprint for Real Pineapple Sherbet, step 1 (see page 60). Allow the syrup to cool completely.

Blend the fruits together, which should make 250 ml/8 fl oz of purée; add an extra kiwi fruit, if necessary, to make up the volume. Stir in the lime juice, then add the cooled syrup. Turn into the ice-cream machine, and freeze-churn until ready to serve.

C A P P U C C I N O

This is strong, refreshing and every bit as good a pick-me-up as the best hot cappuccino.

It also makes a very good filling for a tart (see page 119).

It also makes a very good filling for a tart (see page 119).

INGREDIENTS

INGREDIENTS

40 g/4 Tbsp coarsely ground coffee

600 ml/1 pint hot (not boiling) water

75 g/2³/₄ oz demerara sugar

175 ml/6 fl oz double cream, or a blend of
double and single

grated chocolate and soft brown sugar to decorate

METHOD

Mix the coffee, water and sugar together, stirring until the sugar has
dissolved. Leave until completely cold, then strain.

Stir the cream into the strained coffee, then pour into the ice-cream machine
and freeze-churn until ready to serve.

Serve in cappuccino cups, sprinkled with grated chocolate and brown sugar.

sherbets

$\mathcal{M}$ ANGO

Fully ripe mangoes are one of the most refreshing and exotic fruits;

as a milky sherbet, they make a wonderfully light, low-calorie ice dessert.

INGREDIENTS

125 g/4$^1/_2$ oz caster sugar

600 ml/1 pint milk

1 mango, peeled

juice of half a lemon

1 lime, grated rind and juice

METHOD

Dissolve the sugar in the milk to make a syrup, following the method in the blueprint sherbet, step 1 (see page 60). Allow to cool completely.

Blend the mango flesh with the lemon and lime juices, and the rind of the lime. Add the cold, sweetened milk, then immediately freeze-churn the mixture until ready to serve.

PINK LEMONADE

I use fresh pink lemonade for this recipe, which is coloured with fruit juice.

It makes a very pretty, pink sherbet, which should be served to elegant, elderly aunts in the shade of

a garden parasol. A decoration of a scented geranium leaf would add the finishing touch.

INGREDIENTS

3 large egg whites, whisked

100 g/3¹/₂ oz caster sugar

350 ml/12 fl oz pink lemonade

125 ml/4 fl oz double cream (or a mix of
double and single)

METHOD

Whisk the egg whites and sugar together briefly, until the sugar has dissolved and the egg whites are floppy, not stiff. Stir in the lemonade, followed by the cream.

Turn the sherbet into the ice-cream machine, then freeze-churn until ready to serve.

ASPBERRY

Raspberries are my favourite fruit, and I like them served as plainly as possible. In this sherbet, the flavour of the berries is teamed simply with sugar and cream. What could be better?

175 g/6 oz caster sugar

150 ml/5 fl oz water

350 g/12 oz raspberries

sugar to taste

juice of 1 lemon

2 large egg whites

125 ml/4 fl oz blend of double and single cream

METHOD

Prepare a sugar syrup using the water and sugar; follow the method for the blueprint Real Pineapple Sherbet (see page 60).

Whizz the raspberries in a liquidizer or food processor until smooth. Push the purée through a sieve to remove the tiny seeds. Sweeten to taste with extra sugar; you may need up to 125 g/4½ oz. Stir in the lemon juice.

Continue as for the blueprint, step 2, adding the raspberry purée, the sugar syrup and then the cream. Freeze-churn until ready to serve.

$\mathscr{W}$ATERMELON

Watermelon is the most refreshing melon to use for this sherbet. I have also made it with a canteloupe,

which gave a very delicately flavoured sherbet.

INGREDIENTS

350 ml/12 fl oz milk

75 g/2³/₄ oz caster sugar

300 g/10¹/₂ oz watermelon purée

1 Tbsp lemon juice

METHOD

Prepare a sugar syrup from the milk and sugar following the method for Real Pineapple Sherbet, step 1 (see page 60). Allow to cool completely.

Carefully remove all seeds from the melon, and chop the flesh roughly. Purée until smooth in a liquidizer or food processor, then blend the melon with the sweetened milk and lemon juice. Freeze-churn until ready to serve.

sherbets

GELATOS

blueprint gelato VANILLA POD

ESPRESSO

CHOCOLATE KUMQUAT

CREME BRULEE

JAMAICAN BANANA RUM

MOCHA

CAPPUCCINO

TRIPLE BERRY

DOUBLE NUT

LEMON GRASS & PISTACHIO

An Italian-style ice cream, gelatos are thick and rich, their richness coming not from cream, but from eggs. Usually, it's just the yolks that are used, and up to six may be included in a standard mixture. The resulting ice cream is dense in texture and very intensely flavoured.

Traditional flavours include vanilla, many different types of coffee, soft fruits and nuts. However new flavours are creeping into the gelato range, such as lemon grass and the traditional pistachio, or bananas and rum.

In this chapter I have used the word gelato to include any style of ice cream you might find in an Italian ice-cream parlour. Semifreddo is softer than the traditional gelato, and contains a number of egg whites as well as yolks; I have used this type of mixture for one or two less rich Italian-style ice creams. Unlike sorbets and sherbets, where the egg whites are lightly whipped before mixing, the egg whites in these recipes are whisked until stiff with a small amount of sugar—almost to a soft meringue stage—and are then folded into the mixture just before churning. Freeze-churning for the following recipes will take about 20 minutes, or slightly longer for mixtures containing a large proportion of fruit.

Gelatos freeze well, and can be stored in a suitable covered container in a domestic freezer for up to two months. After this time, especially if you are opening the container and removing scoops, even the richest gelato will begin to form ice crystals, not only on the surface but also within the mixture. Continual tempering and refreezing will also affect the storage time.

Tempering will take 20–30 minutes for a full quantity at room temperature. As with all ice creams, gelatos are at their best when freshly churned, so they should, whenever possible, be eaten straight from your ice-cream maker, or after a brief hardening period in the freezer of 30–60 minutes.

$\mathcal{V}$ANILLA $\mathcal{P}$OD

This vanilla ice dessert has all the richness you would expect from an ice cream. Serve with ripe peaches or apricots, thin sweet biscuits or wafers. Most gelatos are made following this method, although vanilla will not be used in other recipes and should be ignored when following the blueprint for other flavours.

INGREDIENTS

1 large vanilla pod

600 ml/1 pint milk

75 g/2³/₄ oz caster sugar

6 large egg yolks, beaten

½ tsp vanilla extract, or 1 tsp vanilla essence (optional)

METHOD

❶ Carefully split open the vanilla pod with a sharp knife and scrape out the seeds, reserving them for later use. Heat the pod in the milk with the sugar, stirring until dissolved.

❷ Beat the egg yolks until slightly thickened and pale in colour, then pour on the hot milk, beating all the time. Rinse the pan with cold water, return the mixture to it, and heat gently. Stir constantly, until the mixture has thickened sufficiently to just coat the back of a wooden spoon. Remove from the heat, stir in the reserved vanilla seeds, then allow the custard to cool completely.

❸ Remove the vanilla pod (rinse and store for later use), and taste the custard; it should have a really strong vanilla flavour. Add up to half a teaspoon vanilla extract or 1 teaspoon vanilla essence, if necessary, to emphasize the vanilla. Turn the mixture into the machine, and freeze-churn until ready to serve.

$\mathcal{E}$SPRESSO

A richly flavoured coffee ice, perfect for a mid-morning pick-me-up on a hot summer day.

INGREDIENTS

600 ml/1 pint milk

3 Tbsp instant espresso (about 4 individual sachets)

grated rind of half a lemon

10 high roasted coffee beans (e.g. Continental or Italian roast)

1 tsp freshly grated nutmeg (optional)

75 g/2³/₄ oz caster sugar

6 large egg yolks, beaten

METHOD

Heat the milk with the instant espresso, lemon rind, coffee beans, nutmeg (if used) and sugar, stirring until the sugar has dissolved.

Continue by following the blueprint Vanilla Pod recipe, from step 2 (above), but disregard all references to the vanilla. Strain the thickened custard into a bowl before cooling, to remove the coffee beans and lemon rind.

Serve the churned gelato in small scoops.

Vanilla Pod Gelato

CHOCOLATE KUMQUAT

Italian gelatos are often vibrantly fruity. You could use any dessert fruits—apricots, peaches, nectarines or clementines would all work well—but I am suggesting kumquats as most supermarkets now stock them year-round. If you can use local, naturally ripened soft fruits, so much the better.

INGREDIENTS

3 Tbsp unsweetened cocoa powder, sieved

425 ml/15 fl oz milk

1 large or 2 small cinnamon sticks

75 g/2³/₄ oz caster sugar

4 large egg yolks, beaten

1 Tbsp coffee essence, or strong instant coffee

225 g/8 oz kumquats

METHOD

Blend the cocoa to a smooth, thin paste with some of the cold milk, then mix it with the remaining milk in a pan. Heat the milk with the cinnamon and sugar, stirring until the sugar has dissolved.

Continue by following the blueprint Vanilla Pod, from step 2 (see page 72), but beat the egg yolks with the coffee essence. Remove the cinnamon sticks from the custard after cooling.

Wash the kumquats and process them until finely chopped; pieces of peel should still be obvious, but not too large. Mix the kumquats with the cooled chocolate mixture, then turn into the ice-cream machine and freeze-churn until ready to serve.

CREME BRULEE

A smooth vanilla ice cream with crunchy pieces of caramel. This creamy gelato tastes wonderful with fresh fruits marinated in an alcohol sugar syrup—peaches in brandy, for instance, or cherries in Kirsch.

INGREDIENTS

1 large vanilla pod

350 ml/12 fl oz milk

250 ml/9 fl oz single cream

75 g/2³/₄ oz caster sugar

6 large egg yolks, beaten

¹/₂ tsp vanilla extract, or 1 tsp vanilla essence

Caramel

75 g/2³/₄ oz caster sugar

METHOD

Prepare the vanilla custard following the blueprint Vanilla Pod Gelato, steps 1 and 2 (see page 72), then leave it to cool completely.

Prepare the caramel. Slowly heat the remaining sugar in a pan until it has melted, tipping the pan this way and that without stirring the sugar. Continue heating until you achieve a light brown caramel. Pour onto a lightly greased baking sheet, then leave until cold. Chop the caramel finely.

Turn the custard into the ice-cream machine, and freeze-churn until almost ready. Add the chopped caramel, and continue churning until the gelato is ready to serve.

Chocolate Kumquat Gelato

Jamaican Banana Rum Gelato

$\mathcal{J}$AMAICAN $\mathcal{B}$ANANA $\mathcal{R}$UM

Why flavour an Italian-style ice cream with the ingredients of the Caribbean?

Bananas and rum are a winning combination of flavours and textures, so what better reason could there be?

INGREDIENTS

450 ml/15 fl oz milk

1 small cinnamon stick

75 g/2³/₄ oz caster sugar

4 large egg yolks, beaten

2 small ripe bananas

juice of half a lemon

50 g/1³/₄ oz demerara sugar

2–3 Tbsp dark rum

METHOD

Prepare the basic custard as for the blueprint Vanilla Pod Gelato, steps 1 and 2 (see page 72), but heat the cinnamon stick in the milk with the sugar. Remove the cinnamon once the custard has thickened.

Mash the bananas with the lemon juice, brown sugar and rum, then blend with the cooled custard. Turn into the ice-cream machine and freeze-churn until ready to serve.

Try serving with a hot butterscotch sauce and grilled bananas.

$\mathcal{M}$OCHA

The classic combination of chocolate and coffee. Remember to use only coarsely ground coffee or it will be very

difficult to strain the mixture to make a smooth gelato. This recipe contains egg whites, which make it slightly

lighter than many others. The easiest way to chop the chocolate finely is in a food processor.

INGREDIENTS

425 ml/15 fl oz milk

75 g/2³/₄ oz caster sugar

4 Tbsp coarsely ground coffee

1 tsp ground mixed spice

3 large eggs, separated

50 g/1³/₄ oz good-quality chocolate, finely chopped

1 Tbsp caster sugar

METHOD

Heat the milk with the sugar, coffee and spice, then continue to prepare the custard following the blueprint for Vanilla Pod Gelato, step 2 (see page 72). The thickening process will take slightly longer than for most gelatos because there are fewer egg yolks to do the thickening work. Add the finely chopped chocolate to the thickened custard, stir briefly until it has melted, then leave the custard to cool completely.

Whisk the egg whites until thick but not quite stiff, then add the extra sugar and whisk until thoroughly mixed. Add the cold custard and fold the two mixtures together. Pour into the ice-cream machine, then freeze-churn until ready to serve.

CAPPUCCINO

Cinnamon flavours this strong coffee gelato, with grated chocolate stirred into the mixture just before churning

is complete. I grate the chocolate by hand on a coarse grater, to keep some texture in the finished gelato.

INGREDIENTS

425 ml/15 fl oz milk

125 g/4½ oz demerara sugar

3 Tbsp instant espresso coffee
(about 4 individual sachets)

grated rind of half a lemon

1 cinnamon stick

3 large eggs, separated

1 Tbsp caster sugar

2 Tbsp grated chocolate

METHOD

Heat the milk with the demerara sugar, instant espresso, grated lemon rind and the cinnamon stick, then continue following the method for the blueprint Vanilla Pod Gelato, step 2 (see page 72). Thickening the custard may take up to 10 minutes, as there is less egg in this gelato than some others. Remove the cinnamon stick once the custard has cooled completely.

Whisk the egg whites until thick but not quite stiff, then add the sugar and whisk until thoroughly mixed. Add the cold custard and fold the two mixtures together. Freeze-churn until almost firm, then stir in the grated chocolate and continue churning until ready to serve.

TRIPLE BERRY

This very fruity and colourful gelato could also be made with sweet black cherries.

Ideal for serving in crispy sugar cones for a treat any time.

INGREDIENTS

425 ml/15 fl oz milk

75 g/2¾ oz caster sugar

1 tsp vanilla extract, or 2 tsp vanilla essence

5 large egg yolks

200 g/7 oz mixed raspberries, blackberries and
strawberries

2 Tbsp lemon juice

75 g/2¾ oz caster sugar,
to taste

METHOD

Prepare the custard as for the blueprint Vanilla Pod Gelato (see page 72), then leave until completely cold.

Whizz the berries with the lemon juice in a food processor until roughly chopped. Add sufficient extra sugar to sweeten them to your taste; I use about 75 g/2¾ oz. Fold the fruit into the cold custard, then scrape the mixture into the ice-cream machine. Freeze-churn until ready to serve.

Triple Berry Gelato

DOUBLE NUT

Italians often use hazelnuts in their gelatos. I like to toast them, and then to mix them with

some sweetened chestnut purée and a little hazelnut liqueur.

INGREDIENTS

425 ml/15 fl oz milk

75 g/2³/₄ oz caster sugar

1 tsp vanilla extract, or 2 tsp vanilla essence

5 large egg yolks

250 g/9 oz sweetened chestnut purée

2–3 Tbsp hazelnut liqueur or kirsch

50 g/1³/₄ oz toasted hazelnuts, roughly chopped

METHOD

Prepare the custard base for the ice cream by following the blueprint for the Vanilla Pod Gelato (see page 72). Allow the mixture to cool completely.

Beat the chestnut purée with the liqueur, then fold it into the cold custard. Scrape the mixture into the ice-cream machine, and freeze-churn until well thickened. Add the chopped hazelnuts, and continue churning until the gelato is ready to serve.

LEMON GRASS & PISTACHIO

Lemon grass is a hot, sour flavour more usually associated with Thai and Pacific Rim cookery than with

sweet desserts! However, it makes a delicious gelato, clean and refreshing at the end of a meal.

Bruise or flatten the lemon grass with your knife before chopping. For a hotter flavour, chop the thin green

leaves of the lemon grass (if available) into the churned gelato.

Try serving this with warm mince pies or sweet Greek pastries.

INGREDIENTS

600 ml/1 pint milk

75 g/2³/₄ oz caster sugar

1 lemon, grated rind and 1 Tbsp juice

2 large bulbs lemon grass, bruised and finely chopped

6 large egg yolks

50 g/1³/₄ oz pistachios, roughly chopped

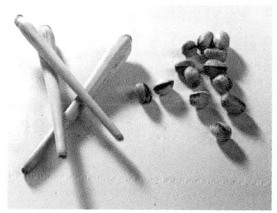

METHOD

Heat the milk with the sugar, lemon rind and lemon grass, then continue preparing the custard following the method for the blueprint for Vanilla Pod Gelato step 2 (see page 72).

Strain the thickened custard to remove the lemon rind and chopped lemon grass, then pour it into the ice-cream machine. Freeze-churn for about 15 minutes until thick, then add the chopped pistachios and lemon grass leaves, if used. Continue churning until the mixture is ready to serve.

I C E   M I L K S

blueprint ice milk VANILLA

CHERRY AMARETTO

DARK SUGAR RIPPLE

CHOCOLATE BUTTERMILK

CHOCOLATE RASPBERRY

RED HOT

MEXICAN CHOCOLATE

CAFE CON LAICHE

DOUBLE CHOCOLATE PEPPERMINT

WHITE CHOCOLATE CHUNK

*Y*ou will have gathered by now that the very best ice creams are loaded with all the things we know to be bad for us in excess—cream and eggs are just the beginning! However, fats are essential for good ice-cream making, since they prevent the frozen product becoming little more than flavoured ice crystals. Take away the fat and storage problems begin.

Ice milks are a good substitute for ice cream, being little more than a frozen, sweetened drink. They are refreshing, a perfect summer cooler, but they must be eaten fresh, preferably straight from the ice-cream machine—well, via a glass or bowl! They will become full of crystals if allowed to start defrosting—which happens very quickly—and then refrozen.

All the recipes in this section are best eaten as soon as freeze-churning is complete; even a short hardening period in the freezer may encourage ice crystals. However, if you wish to serve ice milks in scoops, harden the scoops in the freezer for about an hour, serving them as soon as possible before any ice crystals have a chance to form. Freeze-churning will take about 15 minutes for most of the recipes. If you do freeze these ice creams, you will need to watch them carefully during tempering, as you soften them ready for serving. I suggest allowing about 20–30 minutes in the refrigerator, rather than leaving them at room temperature where they may soften unevenly, the edges melting before the centre has started to defrost.

If you are trying hard to diet, remember that even the ice milk recipes in this chapter contain a lot of sugar. In dietary terms, ice milks are the good guys, full-fat ice creams are utterly sinful, and reduced-fat ice creams are just wicked!

VANILLA

This basic recipe has a really good flavour. It is simple and relatively quick to make, and is best served freshly churned. The salt in this recipe helps to emphasize the flavour of the other ingredients.

INGREDIENTS

850 ml/1¹/₂ pints milk

125 g/4¹/₂ oz caster sugar

1 tsp vanilla extract, or 2 tsp vanilla essence

pinch of salt

METHOD

❶ Heat the milk until almost boiling, when tiny bubbles are just rising to the surface. Add the sugar and stir until dissolved, then leave the milk to cool completely.

❷ Stir the vanilla and salt into the cold milk, then pour it into the ice-cream machine. Freeze-churn until thick and ready to serve.

CHERRY AMARETTO

For a special treat, steep the cherries in a tablespoon or two of Kirsch or Amaretto liqueur before adding them, but remember that alcohol, like anything enjoyable, does contain calories.

INGREDIENTS

850 ml/1¹/₂ pints milk

125 g/4¹/₂ oz caster sugar

1 tsp vanilla extract, or 2 tsp vanilla essence

pinch of salt

75 g/2³/₄ oz cherries, roughly chopped

50 g/1³/₄ oz amaretti biscuits, roughly chopped

METHOD

Prepare the basic ice milk following the blueprint recipe for Vanilla Ice Milk (above).

Freeze-churn the cooled mixture until almost ready to serve, then scoop it out of the ice-cream machine into a bowl. Fold in the chopped cherries and biscuits, then allow the mixture to harden slightly in the freezer for 10–15 minutes before serving.

Cherry Amaretto Ice Milk

Dark Sugar Ripple Ice Milk

DARK SUGAR RIPPLE

This is not flavoured with a true praline, but the simple addition of molasses sugar, swirled through the ice milk, gives a flavour not far short of the real thing. The effect is an abstract ripple, the sugar melting unevenly. However, as this type of ice milk is best churned and eaten immediately, it is the quickest and most convenient way of including a ripple effect.

INGREDIENTS

850 ml/1½ pints milk

125 g/4½ oz caster sugar

1 tsp vanilla extract, or 2 tsp vanilla essence

pinch of salt

1–2 Tbsp dark molasses sugar

METHOD

Prepare the basic ice milk following the blueprint for Vanilla Ice Milk (see page 84).

Freeze-churn the ice milk until ready to serve. Scoop the mixture into a serving bowl, scattering the molasses sugar over the ice milk as you build up the dessert in the bowl. Leave to stand for 2-3 minutes before serving, so that the sugar begins to run or ripple through the mixture. Alternatively, harden scoops of the ice milk for about an hour before serving.

CHOCOLATE BUTTERMILK

Buttermilk adds a definite piquancy to the flavour of ices, making them more robust and slightly yogurty. The buttermilk combines very well with chocolate. I prefer this ice milk not too sweet, but you can vary the amount of sugar to suit your personal taste.

INGREDIENTS

75 g/2¾ oz caster sugar, or to taste

2 Tbsp unsweetened cocoa powder, sieved

125 ml/4 fl oz milk

350 ml/12 fl oz buttermilk

½ tsp vanilla extract, or 1 tsp vanilla essence

METHOD

Blend the sugar and cocoa with a little of the cold milk. Heat the remaining milk until almost boiling, then pour it onto the cocoa and stir until the sugar has dissolved. Leave the flavoured milk until completely cold.

Beat the buttermilk and vanilla together until smooth, then fold in the cold chocolate mixture. Freeze-churn until ready to serve. This ice milk should be served freshly churned, but is slightly better for freezing than many other reduced-fat varieties, should you need to make it in advance.

CHOCOLATE RASPBERRY

There are two ways to make a good chocolate and raspberry ice milk. Either add chopped chocolate to the basic vanilla recipe with the raspberry purée, or make a chocolate base, which is what I prefer to do.

INGREDIENTS

3 Tbsp unsweetened cocoa powder, sieved

600 ml/1 pint milk

125 g/4½ oz caster sugar

1 tsp vanilla extract, or 2 tsp vanilla essence

125 g/4½ oz raspberries

grated rind and juice of half a lemon

sugar to taste

METHOD

Blend the cocoa to a thin paste with a little of the cold milk. Heat the remaining milk with the sugar until the sugar has dissolved and the milk is almost boiling. Add the hot milk to the cocoa, stirring all the time. Flavour with the vanilla, then leave until completely cold.

Whizz the raspberries with the lemon rind and juice in a food processor, and add sufficient sugar to sweeten them to taste. Rub the purée through a sieve, if you wish, then chill it until required.

Turn the chocolate milk into the ice-cream machine and freeze-churn until ready to serve. Remove the dasher from the machine, pressing the ice milk back into the machine. Make some holes in the ice milk, using a thick skewer or a thin spoon handle, and fill with the raspberry purée. Leave for a few minutes, then scoop out the ice milk across the purée, creating a ripple effect. Alternatively, drizzle the purée over the chocolate ice milk as you scoop it.

RED HOT

An ice with a kick! Who needs the richness of a full-fat ice cream when you have this stunning combination of flavours—cool, exotic mango and red-hot chilli?

INGREDIENTS

425 ml/15 fl oz milk

1–2 dried red chillies, according to your sense of adventure

1 large ripe mango

1 Tbsp lemon juice

1 large egg

100 g/3½ oz caster sugar

1 habanero chilli, finely chopped (optional)

METHOD

Heat the milk with the dried chilli until almost boiling, then remove the pan from the heat and leave until completely cold. Discard the chilli.

Trim the flesh of the mango away from the stone and peel it. Whizz the mango with the lemon juice to a purée; you should have about 125 g/4½ oz.

Whisk the egg and sugar until thick and pale. Fold in the purée, then gradually whisk in the milk. Turn into the ice-cream machine, and freeze-churn until almost ready to serve. Add the chopped habanero, if desired, and continue churning until it is evenly mixed into the ice milk. Serve immediately.

Red Hot Ice Milk

MEXICAN CHOCOLATE

Strongly flavoured with cinnamon, this is an ideal ice milk to serve with an exotic fruit salad

or some fresh sliced papaya.

INGREDIENTS

3 Tbsp unsweetened cocoa powder, sieved

125 g/4¹/₂ oz caster sugar

2 large cinnamon sticks

600 ml/1 pint milk

1 large egg white

40 g/1¹/₂ oz pecan nuts,

chopped

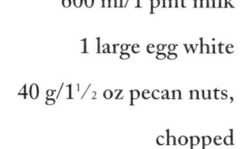

METHOD

Blend the cocoa and sugar to a thin paste with a little of the cold milk. Whisk in the remaining milk, then heat gently with the cinnamon sticks until the sugar has dissolved. Remove the pan from the heat, and leave until completely cold. Discard the cinnamon.

Lightly beat the egg white until very frothy, then add the cold milk. Turn into the ice-cream machine, and freeze-churn until almost ready to serve. Add the chopped pecans, and continue churning for a few more minutes.

CAFE CON LECHE

This sweet, creamy coffee ice milk is made with evaporated milk, which gives a luxurious flavour.

INGREDIENTS

125 ml/4 fl oz milk

40 g/4 Tbsp coarsely ground coffee

100 g/3¹/₂ oz demerara sugar

410 g/14 oz can evaporated milk

1 large egg white

METHOD

Heat the milk until almost boiling, then pour it onto the coffee and sugar. Stir until the sugar has dissolved, then strain the coffee into a clean bowl. Add the evaporated milk, and leave until completely cold.

Whisk the egg white until frothy, then gradually add the coffee mixture and continue whisking until thoroughly combined. Turn into the ice-cream machine, and freeze-churn until ready to serve.

Mexican Chocolate Ice Milk

DOUBLE CHOCOLATE PEPPERMINT

A chocolate and peppermint treat that can be made even more special by adding 1–2 tablespoons of crème de menthe, if you wish.

INGREDIENTS

3 Tbsp unsweetened cocoa powder, sieved

125 g/4½ oz caster sugar

600 ml/1 pint milk

1 tsp vanilla extract, or 2 tsp vanilla essence

1–2 Tbsp crème de menthe (optional)

50 g/1¾ oz peppermint creams, chopped

25 g/1 oz chocolate chips, roughly cut

METHOD

Blend the cocoa and sugar to a thin paste with a little of the cold milk, then add the remaining milk and continue as for the blueprint Vanilla Ice Milk (see page 84), adding the vanilla flavouring to the hot milk. Add the crème de menthe to the milk when completely cold, if desired.

Freeze-churn until thick, then add the chopped peppermint creams and the chocolate chips. Continue to churn until the ice milk is ready to serve.

*W*HITE *C*HOCOLATE *C*HUNK

White chocolate is much sweeter than milk or dark chocolate, so I use a little less sugar in this recipe than in many others. The basic mixture is flavoured with white chocolate, and chips of white and dark chocolate are added at the end.

INGREDIENTS

600 ml/1 pint milk

50 g/1³/₄ oz caster sugar

100 g/3¹/₂ oz white chocolate, roughly chopped

1 tsp vanilla extract, or 2 tsp vanilla essence

pinch of salt

50 g/1³/₄ oz white chocolate chips, roughly chopped

25 g/1 oz dark chocolate chips, roughly chopped

METHOD

Prepare the basic ice milk following the blueprint for Vanilla Ice Milk (see page 84), adding the chopped white chocolate to the hot milk and stirring until it has melted. The finer you chop the chocolate, the quicker this will be; using a food processor is ideal. Leave the mixture until completely cold.

Stir in the vanilla and salt, then turn into the ice-cream machine. Freeze-churn until the mixture is thick, then add the roughly cut chocolate chips and continue churning until ready to serve.

FROZEN YOGURT
& TOFU ICE CREAM

blueprint frozen yogurt VANILLA

blueprint luxury frozen yogurt LUXURY LEMON

DOUBLE GINGER

NECTARINE

BLUEBERRY LEMON

RASPBERRY

MINTED PINEAPPLE

DOUBLE CHOCOLATE

STRAWBERRY

RASPBERRY & VANILLA TOFU RIPPLE

CHOCOLATE TOFU WITH CHERRIES & HAZELNUTS

*F*rozen yogurts are probably just about the quickest of all ice creams to make. For the ultimate quick cheat, you could even freeze a commercial fruit yogurt, but I really think the following ideas are worth the little extra effort required!

If you are a yogurt fanatic, you may like to prepare the recipes using a home-made yogurt base; if you make your yogurt with cream, you will have a deliciously rich result. However, I have used the standard low-fat yogurt in all the following recipes, except where stated, and have had wonderful results.

Frozen yogurts do not require heating, since this often causes the yogurt to split. You should, however, thoroughly beat the sugar into the yogurt to ensure it has dissolved into the mixture. Some people like to use honey in place of sugar as they find it easier to combine with the yogurt. I like frozen fruit yogurts best, but chocolate also combines well.

You can add cream to frozen yogurt to enrich the mixture. I sometimes add egg whites, making them into a soft meringue to use as the base; this makes for a very rich, luxurious yogurt dessert. Fruit juices and purées should be added to frozen yogurts just before churning but since most recipes are as straightforward as mix and churn, this is somewhat elementary.

The frozen yogurts require approximately 15–20 minutes to freeze-churn until ready for serving. They are perfect for serving straight from the ice-cream machine, but may be hardened in scoops or stored in the freezer for a short time. I would not recommend storing frozen yogurt for longer than one month, in case it forms ice crystals and starts to deteriorate.

VANILLA

A perfect ice dessert to make when you are in a hurry. There is no heating or cooling;

just mix all the ingredients together, then freeze-churn. I find this recipe increases in bulk considerably

during churning, so don't be tempted to add more ingredients than the recipe states.

INGREDIENTS

350 g/12 oz natural yogurt

200 ml/6 fl oz double cream

75 g/2³/₄ oz caster sugar

1 tsp vanilla extract, or 2 tsp vanilla essence

METHOD

① Beat all the ingredients together until smooth, then turn them into the ice-cream machine.

② Freeze-churn until ready to serve.

LUXURY LEMON

This is a creamy, luxurious frozen yogurt, but the clean tang of yogurt lurking in the background makes you

believe that it is a diet dessert. Have everything ready and weighed out before you begin the sugar syrup and

the meringue, since you need to keep whisking to cool the mixture quickly.

INGREDIENTS

150 g/5¹/₂ oz caster sugar

6 Tbsp water

2 large egg whites

pinch of salt

150 g/5¹/₂ oz natural yogurt

2 lemons, finely grated rind and juice

250 ml/9 fl oz double cream

METHOD

① Dissolve the sugar in the water and bring slowly to the boil. Simmer for three minutes.

② Meanwhile, whisk the egg whites with the salt until stiff.

③ Gradually pour the syrup onto the egg whites, whisking all the time, and continue whisking for 2–3 minutes. Add the yogurt, and continue to whisk until the mixture is cool. Whisk in the finely grated lemon rind and the lemon juice, then fold in the cream.

④ Scrape the mixture into the ice-cream machine, and freeze-churn until ready to serve.

Luxury Lemon Frozen Yogurt

DOUBLE GINGER

The heat of ginger with the chill of a frozen dessert is always a winning combination. The chopped ginger gives wonderful bursts of flavour, and the yogurt is extra delicious when served with a thick chocolate sauce. This is a meringue-based frozen yogurt, so have all the ingredients weighed out and ready before you start.

INGREDIENTS

150 g/5^{1}/$_{2}$ oz caster sugar

2 tsp ground ginger

6 Tbsp water

2 large egg whites

pinch of salt

150 g/5^{1}/$_{2}$ oz natural yogurt

250 ml/9 fl oz double cream

60 g/2 oz crystallized or preserved ginger, chopped

METHOD

Dissolve the sugar with the ground ginger in the water, then continue following the blueprint for Luxury Lemon Frozen Yogurt, from step 1 (see page 96).

Add the chopped ginger to the mixture once it has started to thicken during churning. Continue churning until it is ready to serve.

frozen yogurts

ℕECTARINE

The sweet freshness of nectarines blends well with the flavour and texture of yogurt to give a light,

refreshing ice. A perfect ice for serving with rhubarb tart or plum compôte.

200 g/7 oz roughly puréed nectarines,
about 4 medium fruits

1 Tbsp lemon juice

100 g/3½ oz caster sugar

575 g/20 oz natural yogurt

METHOD

Beat all the ingredients together until smooth. Spoon into the ice-cream machine, then freeze-churn until ready to serve.

ℬLUEBERRY ℒEMON

Delicious, and colourful too! I add the blueberries to the half-frozen mixture, and then finish the hardening in the freezer to keep the pieces of fruit defined in the ice. Try serving with freshly baked muffins.

INGREDIENTS

350 g/12 oz natural yogurt

200 ml/6 fl oz double cream, or a blend of single and double

75 g/2³/₄ oz caster sugar

1 tsp vanilla extract, or 2 tsp vanilla essence

1 lemon, grated rind and juice

125 g/4¹/₂ oz blueberries

METHOD

Beat all the ingredients, except the blueberries, together in a large bowl until smooth. Turn into the ice-cream machine, and freeze-churn until thick.

Meanwhile, roughly chop or blend the blueberries, leaving some pieces of fruit in the mixture. Transfer the yogurt ice to a bowl, then fold in the blueberries. Pile into a suitable covered container, and freeze for 30 minutes before serving.

ℛASPBERRY

A meringue-based frozen yogurt is a wonderful way to serve my favourite berries, with either a raspberry purée or some lightly stewed fruits.

INGREDIENTS

225 g/8 oz raspberries

grated rind and juice of half a lemon

150 g/5¹/₂ oz caster sugar

6 Tbsp water

2 large egg whites

pinch of salt

150 g/5¹/₂ oz natural yogurt

250 ml/9 fl oz double cream

1 tsp vanilla extract, or 2 tsp vanilla essence

METHOD

Whizz the raspberries with the lemon rind and juice in a liquidizer or food processor until puréed. Press the mixture through a sieve with the back of a ladle to remove all the seeds, then leave until required.

Prepare the yogurt mixture following the blueprint for Luxury Lemon Frozen Yogurt (see page 96). Fold in the raspberry purée with the vanilla extract and cream at step 4, then spoon into the ice-cream machine and freeze-churn until ready to serve.

Blueberry Lemon Frozen Yogurt

MINTED PINEAPPLE

I think applemint is the best variety for cooking. It is not too sharp, and does what all good seasonings

should do: it enhances the flavour of the main ingredient without dominating it.

INGREDIENTS

350 g/12 oz natural yogurt

200 ml/6 fl oz double cream

75 g/2³/₄ oz caster sugar

1 tsp vanilla extract, or 2 tsp vanilla essence

225 g/8 oz crushed pineapple, thoroughly drained

1–2 Tbsp fresh applemint or

pineapple mint, chopped

mint sprigs to decorate

METHOD

Beat all the ingredients together until smooth. Turn into the ice-cream machine, then freeze-churn until ready to serve.

DOUBLE CHOCOLATE

Chocolate-flavoured yogurt is very popular, but I am only happy with the combination if I use

good-quality cocoa or chocolate. I also like to add some chocolate chips for extra texture.

This frozen yogurt requires hot milk to bring out the flavour of the cocoa.

INGREDIENTS

25 g/1 oz unsweetened cocoa powder, sieved

100 g/3¹/₂ oz caster sugar

250 ml/9 fl oz milk

450 g/1 lb natural yogurt

125 ml/4 fl oz double cream

75 g/2³/₄ oz roughly chopped chocolate chips

METHOD

Blend the cocoa and sugar to a paste with a little of the cold milk. Heat the remaining milk until almost boiling, then pour it onto the cocoa and stir until the sugar has dissolved. Allow to cool completely.

Add the yogurt and cream, stir well, then pour the mixture into the ice-cream machine. Freeze-churn until thick, then add the chocolate chips and continue churning until ready to serve.

Minted Pineapple Frozen Yogurt

STRAWBERRY

Fresh, ripe strawberries are the perfect fruit for using in any iced dessert. Do not use fruits

that have been frozen, as they will become too watery and then icy when refrozen;

canned strawberries lack both the colour and texture of the fresh fruits.

INGREDIENTS

METHOD

225 g/8 oz strawberries

grated rind and juice of half a lemon

100 g/3$\frac{1}{2}$ oz caster sugar

575 g/20 oz natural yogurt

1 tsp vanilla extract, or 2 tsp vanilla essence

Whizz the strawberries with the lemon rind and juice in a liquidizer or food processor. Leave the purée slightly rough in texture.

Beat the purée with the remaining ingredients, then freeze-churn. Serve straight from the ice-cream machine, as the pieces of strawberry may become icy if stored in the freezer.

RASPBERRY & VANILLA TOFU RIPPLE

This is an excellent recipe for anyone with a dairy products intolerance, as it uses not only tofu

but soya milk as well. I find it easier to get a ripple effect by packing the basic ice cream into a freezer

container, drizzling the fruit purée over the mixture as I gradually pack it in.

INGREDIENTS

METHOD

125 g/4$\frac{1}{2}$ oz raspberries

grated rind and juice of half a lemon

570 g/19 oz plain tofu

200 g/7 oz clear honey

1 tsp vanilla extract, or 2 tsp vanilla essence

250 ml/9 fl oz soya milk

Whizz the raspberries with the lemon rind and juice in a liquidizer or food processor. Press the purée through a sieve with the back of a ladle to remove the seeds, then reserve the purée until required.

Rinse the processor, then whizz the remaining ingredients together until smooth. Turn into the ice-cream machine and freeze-churn for 20–25 minutes, until ready to serve.

Pack the tofulatto into a freezer container, drizzling the raspberry purée over it as you go. Freeze until required.

CHOCOLATE TOFU WITH CHERRIES & HAZELNUTS

Tofu may seem like a strange ingredient to use as the base of an iced dessert, but it works extremely well. If you are preparing this for someone following a special diet, you may need to substitute carob for the chocolate, especially if your guest has a dairy products intolerance. The egg yolks give extra body to the mixture but may be omitted.

INGREDIENTS

200 g/7 oz good-quality chocolate, broken into pieces

570 g/19 oz plain tofu

175 g/6 oz caster sugar

2 tsp coffee essence or strong instant coffee

4 large egg yolks

4 Tbsp brandy

canned black cherries or fresh cherries

chopped toasted hazelnuts

METHOD

Melt the chocolate slowly, either in a heavy-based pan, in a bowl over a pan of water or in a microwave oven. Allow it to cool slightly.

Blend all the remaining ingredients except the cherries and hazelnuts together in a processor or liquidizer, then add the cooled chocolate and blend again. Turn the mixture into an ice-cream machine, and freeze-churn for 10–15 minutes.

Serve the tofu latto in scoops over cherries in a glass dish, topped with chopped nuts.

SAUCES

CHOCOLATE ORANGE

HOT CHOCOLATE FUDGE

BITTERSWEET CHOCOLATE

HOT RUM SABAYON

HOT CARAMEL

BUTTERSCOTCH

RASPBERRY MARSHMALLOW

MANGO

FRESH PINEAPPLE & KIWI

CHERRY JUBILEE

*G*lance along the shelves in almost any supermarket and you will be overwhelmed by the sauces available to decorate, cajole and generally excite ice creams. Although I heartily applaud the variety on offer, I suggest a note of caution. They are usually made with flavourings rather than the Real Thing—chocolate flavoured instead of chocolate sauce, maple syrup flavoured instead of real maple syrup. Certainly, if you are making your own ice creams, you should make your own toppings.

If you want a quick topping, there are many options that involve no cooking at all: fruit syrups and drinks such as crème de cassis, grenadine or sloe gin provide a splash of excitement, and dry vermouth is absolutely wonderful on sorbets. Cream liqueurs, with or without a sprinkling of chopped nuts, add an extra touch of luxury to coffee or chocolate ice creams; serve an ice cream topped with coffee cream liqueur in Irish whiskey glasses for a simple but stylish dessert.

Maple syrup can be spooned over ice cream for the ultimate quick sauce. It is a mild, delicate but perfect partner for many flavours, including crème brulée, coffee, vanilla and the many ices that include exotic fruits such as mango.

Quick hot sauces can be made in a number of ways. Try melting jam and adding the juice of a lemon or orange, or heating chocolate bars slowly to make the easiest of fudge sauces. Luxury cranberry sauces, especially those that include orange, also make a good topping when heated gently.

There are several ways of making speedy fresh fruit sauces, the easiest of which is to whizz fresh fruits in a food processor with sugar to taste. Sieve the sauce, if it is necessary to remove seeds, and then serve. Icing sugar dissolves quickly into the fruit but I often think granulated sugar gives a slightly clearer sauce.

All the recipes in this chapter will serve about six people.

CHOCOLATE ORANGE

Probably my all-time favourite sauce for ice cream. Use evaporated milk if you prefer, but I like to stir cream into the sauce for complete and utter decadence.

INGREDIENTS

200 g/7 oz bitter chocolate (use chips or a bar broken into small squares)

3 Tbsp golden syrup

1 Tbsp butter

150 ml/5 fl oz single cream

1 orange, grated rind and juice

2–3 Tbsp orange liqueur, e.g. Cointreau

METHOD

This sauce may be made in a microwave or in a bowl over a pan of hot water. Heat the chocolate, syrup and butter together until melted, then stir in the cream and whisk until thoroughly mixed. Add the orange rind and juice, and the liqueur, then use as required.

Hot Chocolate Fudge

A very quick and easy sauce, which must be used straight away—partly because it thickens in the fridge, and partly because it is too tempting to eat by the spoonful!

INGREDIENTS

150 g/5¹/₂ oz good dark chocolate, broken into small pieces

3 Tbsp golden syrup

1 tsp coffee essence (optional)

5 Tbsp hot water

METHOD

Heat the chocolate, syrup and coffee essence together in a heavy-based pan until the chocolate has melted. Stir in the hot water, then remove from the heat and beat thoroughly for a few seconds until smooth. Serve immediately over the ice cream of your choice.

Bittersweet Chocolate

A mixture of milk and plain chocolate in a creamy sauce sweetened with a little honey makes a wonderful bittersweet chocolate topping.

INGREDIENTS

125 ml/4 fl oz single cream

2 Tbsp clear honey

75 g/2³/₄ oz fine plain chocolate, finely chopped

75 g/2³/₄ oz milk chocolate, finely chopped

1 tsp unsalted butter

¹/₂ tsp vanilla extract, or 1 tsp vanilla essence

METHOD

Heat the cream and honey gently until blended together. Add in the chocolate and the butter, and continue stirring over a low heat until the chocolate has melted and all the ingredients have combined together. Add the vanilla, then serve the sauce warm.

HOT RUM SABAYON

This sounds exotic, and it is. It is also very sweet, so don't be over-generous with the portions!

It is terrific with all chocolate, rum and coffee ice creams, as well as those flavoured with fruits.

INGREDIENTS

40 g/1¹/₂ oz unsalted butter, softened

125 g/4¹/₂ oz light soft brown sugar

1 large egg, separated

3 Tbsp rum

METHOD

Heat the butter, sugar and egg yolk in a bowl over a pan of hot (not boiling) water. Stir the mixture almost constantly to ensure the egg does not start to curdle. Continue stirring the mixture over a gentle heat until the sugar has dissolved and the mixture has thickened.

Whisk the egg white until stiff, then fold it into the hot buttery mixture with the rum. Serve immediately.

HOT CARAMEL

This is a very thin caramel that will not become brittle, making it an ideal topping sauce.

Carefully add hot water to the caramel, and I suggest you wear oven gloves just in case the caramel spits.

Add the hot water very slowly and there should be no problem.

INGREDIENTS

150 ml/5 fl oz water

75 g/2³/₄ oz caster sugar

200 ml/7 fl oz hot water

juice of half a lemon

METHOD

Heat the cold water and sugar together very gently until the sugar has dissolved; stir the mixture with a metal spoon to ensure there are no sugar crystals remaining. Bring the syrup to the boil, then cook the caramel until it is golden brown, without stirring.

Remove the pan from the heat and add the hot water very gradually, stirring to mix it into the caramel. Strain the lemon juice into the sauce, then reheat it gently, if necessary, before serving.

Hot Rum Sabayon Sauce

$\mathcal{B}$UTTERSCOTCH

Another of my favourites, this sauce is especially good with banana or caramel ice creams.

50 g/1¾ oz butter

50 g/1¾ oz demerara sugar

2 Tbsp golden syrup

125 ml/4 fl oz milk

METHOD

Heat the butter, sugar and syrup together in a small, heavy-based pan until the butter has melted and the ingredients have blended together. Boil rapidly until the mixture is at 115°C/235°F, soft ball stage (this should be marked on your sugar thermometer). Cool the mixture slightly, then gradually beat in the milk. Use warm, or cool completely.

$\mathcal{R}$ASPBERRY $\mathcal{M}$ARSHMALLOW

For those with a sweet tooth and an eye for colour! This sauce would be just as good made with strawberries

or blueberries; use your favourite fruit. I like to serve this sauce warm, but it is really just as good cold.

INGREDIENTS

125 g/4^{1}/$_{2}$ oz fresh raspberries

50 g/1^{3}/$_{4}$ oz icing sugar, sieved

50 ml/2 fl oz water

10–12 marshmallows

METHOD

Whizz the raspberries and the sugar in a food processor until smooth, then press through a sieve to remove the seeds.

Heat the fruit purée with the water until almost at the boil, then add the marshmallows and remove the pan from the heat. Stir the sauce until the marshmallows have melted, then beat thoroughly with a wooden spoon until they are blended into the fruit. Serve warm or cold.

$\mathcal{M}$ANGO

I have combined fresh mango and ginger to produce a velvety smooth fruit sauce that will

enrobe itself around scoops of ice cream.

INGREDIENTS

2 large, ripe mangoes

1 lemon, grated rind and juice

5 cm/2 in piece fresh root ginger

1 tsp ground ginger

50 g/1^{3}/$_{4}$ oz sieved icing sugar, or to taste

METHOD

Cut the mango cheeks away from the stones of the fruits, then peel them and trim away any extra flesh around the stones. Place the fruit in a liquidizer or food processor with the lemon rind and juice. Grate the ginger, including the skin, then squeeze the juice from the shreds over the mango. Discard the shreds. Add the ground ginger and icing sugar, then whizz until smooth. Add extra sugar, if necessary, and whizz again.

Press the purée through a sieve using the back of a ladle; it should be thick enough to coat the back of a spoon. Serve over scoops of ice cream.

FRESH PINEAPPLE & KIWI FRUIT

I really like this combination of fruits, but you could make a plain pineapple sauce, following exactly the same

method. Use over other exotic fruit sherbets or sorbets, or with vanilla, rum or caramel ice creams. Canned

crushed pineapple may also be used for the sauce, but the flavour will not be so sharp.

INGREDIENTS

150 g/5½ oz fresh pineapple purée

2 kiwi fruits, peeled and chopped

40 g/1½ oz caster sugar, to taste

2 Tbsp maple syrup

METHOD

Blend the kiwi fruits and sugar with the pineapple purée until smooth, then add the maple syrup. Serve hot or cold; warm the sauce gently until almost boiling to serve hot.

CHERRY JUBILEE

This is my version of a sauce that is something of a classic—and what could be more impressive than a flambéed sauce to serve with ice cream? Don't be tempted to spoon it over the ice cream before lighting the brandy as it will probably go straight out, if it lights at all. It is far more reliable to light the sauce in a suitable sauceboat.

250 g/9 oz canned stoned black cherries

2 level tsp arrowroot

250 ml/9 fl oz juice from the canned cherries

juice of half a lemon

50 ml/2 fl oz brandy

METHOD

Drain the cherries, reserving the juice from the can, then cut the fruits in half. Blend the arrowroot with the measured juice, then heat gently in a small saucepan until boiling, when the sauce will clear. Stir in the cherries with the lemon juice, and cook for a further one minute, to heat the fruits.

Pour the sauce into a warmed sauceboat or serving dish. Warm the brandy; the easiest way to do this is in a metal ladle over the heat. Pour the brandy over the sauce and light it immediately with a match.

Serve the cherry sauce over ice cream once the flames have subsided.

sauces

DESSERTS

ORANGE CHOCOLATE-CHIP MILLE FEUILLE WITH
BANANAS & HOT RUM SABAYON SAUCE

CAPPUCCINO TART

MILE-HIGH ICE-CREAM PIE

MISSISSIPPI MUD PIE

PEACH MELBA

TOOTI FRUITI BOMBE

CHOCOLATE ICE-CREAM ROULADE

HOOLIGAN'S SOUP

All the ice creams in this book make wonderful desserts just as they are, or with the fresh fruits, toppings or sauce of your choice. Most, however, can also be made into fully fledged ice-cream desserts, becoming even more luscious for serving at supper parties, on birthdays and at other important events.

The following are some of my favourites, but they are really just to start you off, a point of reference from which you will be able to create your own ice-cream confections. Chocolate features largely in my selection. This may be due to my own personal preference (willingly confessed) or to the fact that many of my friends are also addicted to it. Justification is not necessary—good-quality chocolate turns most desserts into a treat!

Use freshly churned ice creams for these desserts, or some which have been made in advance and stored in the freezer. I find that the ices are at the correct consistency for "doing things with" immediately after churning, so frozen ice creams will need to be softened a little or tempered before use, especially if they are to be reshaped or moulded. Remember that if you are building up a large volume of ice cream in a dessert, for example in a bombe, the dessert will need a considerable time to freeze properly, so that all the layers are of the same consistency when it's time to serve.

Not all the desserts in this chapter will require a full quantity of ice cream, but there is little point in making up less than the standard recipe. You will have to use your own judgment as to exactly how much you can pack into your flan case or bombe mould. Devour any leftovers as a cook's perk, or freeze in a small container for days when only one or two portions of ice cream are required.

Orange Chocolate-Chip Mille Feuille With Bananas & Hot Rum Sabayon Sauce

I use a colourful orange sherbet to fill this light, flaky pastry dessert, but a raspberry or tropical fruit sherbet would work just as well.

INGREDIENTS

Orange Chocolate Chip Sherbet (see page 60)

1 x 275 g/9½ oz packet puff pastry (defrosted if previously frozen)

sieved icing sugar to serve

2 large bananas

Hot Rum Sabayon Sauce (see page 110)

METHOD ◇ SERVES 6 - 8

Prepare the sherbet following the recipe on page 60. Line a large loaf tin with cling film and turn half the sherbet into it, once freeze-churning is complete. Cover with more cling film, then spoon in the remaining sherbet. Harden the mixture for 45 minutes in the freezer, or until required.

Preheat the oven to 220°C/425°F/Gas Mark 7. Roll out the pastry until just large enough to cut into 3 rectangles the same size as the loaf tin. Trim the edges of the pastry, cut out the rectangles, then transfer them to a lightly greased baking sheet, side by side but not touching. Prick the pastry thoroughly all over, then bake in the preheated oven for 15 minutes, until crisp and golden brown. Transfer to a wire rack to cool.

Prepare the Sabayon Sauce to the stage where the egg yolks and sugar have thickened (see page 110). Keep the sauce warm, or start to reheat it over a bowl of hot water while assembling the pastry slice.

Keep the most perfect piece of pastry for the top of the Mille Feuille. Cut each of the remaining pieces into the number of slices required (this will make serving the finished dish much easier).

Arrange one set of pastry pieces on a serving plate, then top with one part of the hardened sherbet. Cover with the remaining pastry pieces, lining them up carefully so that the knife can just glide through when serving. Lay the last piece of sherbet over the top, then finish off with the reserved pastry slice. Dredge lightly with sieved icing sugar, then slice and arrange on plates.

Cut the bananas into slices, then arrange two or three pieces on each plate. Caramelize them slightly by dredging them with icing sugar and then placing a very hot skewer on each slice for a few seconds.

Finish the Sabayon Sauce quickly by folding in the rum and the whisked egg whites. Spoon the sauce around the Mille Feuille and serve immediately, with any extra sauce in a warmed jug.

CAPPUCCINO TART

This tart is lighter than most since the filling is a sherbet, not a rich ice cream. Topped with lightly whipped cream and flaked chocolate, it is the type of cappuccino that dreams are made of!

INGREDIENTS

Cappuccino Sherbet (see page 65)

100 g/3½ oz butter

225 g/8 oz crushed chocolate digestive biscuits

1 tsp caster sugar

300 ml/10 fl oz double cream

flaked chocolate and coffee sugar crystals to decorate

METHOD ◇ SERVES 8

Freeze-churn the sherbet, or soften a previously frozen batch for 15 minutes.

Melt the butter then add the biscuit crumbs and sugar, off the heat, stirring until well mixed. Press the crumbs evenly over the base and sides of a 23 cm/ 9 in metal flan tin with a removable base. Chill until required.

Fill the biscuit base with the sherbet, then harden it in the freezer for at least 30 minutes. Temper the tart in the fridge for 15 minutes before serving if frozen for one hour or longer, removing the flan tin as soon as possible.

Whip the cream until just thick enough to hold its shape. Pile the cream over the sherbet just before serving, forking it up into soft peaks. Scatter flaked chocolate and a little sugar over the cream, then serve immediately.

Mile-High Ice-Cream Pie

This dessert is for those who don't want last-minute panics when they are cooking!

The meringue for this dessert is frozen, so the whole thing may be prepared several days in advance.

If you really want to impress your guests, you may like to fill the biscuit case with a double quantity of ice

cream or frozen yogurt—it's up to you. If you do, increase the meringue ingredients to 4 egg whites and

225 g/8 oz caster sugar, and double the amount of fruit.

INGREDIENTS

Strawberry Ice Cream (see page 36) or Raspberry
Frozen Yogurt (see page 100)

100 g/3¹/₂ oz butter

225 g/8 oz crushed chocolate digestive biscuits

1 tsp caster sugar

175 g/6 oz strawberries or raspberries, roughly
chopped

2 large egg whites

pinch of salt

125 g/4¹/₂ oz caster sugar

1 tsp cream of tartar

METHOD ◇ SERVES 8

Prepare the chosen ice cream and freeze-churn it. Melt the butter, then add in the digestive biscuit crumbs and sugar and mix thoroughly. Press into an 20 cm/8 in ovenproof ceramic dish, and chill until the ice cream or yogurt is churned.

Mix the fruit into the ice cream, then pack it into the digestive biscuit base, mounding it up in the centre. Harden the pie in the freezer for 1–1¹/₂ hours.

Preheat your oven to its hottest setting (not the grill). Whisk the egg whites with the salt until stiff, then gradually add the sugar and cream of tartar, whisking all the time, until the meringue is stiff and glossy. Do not overbeat the egg whites once you have added the sugar.

Pile the meringue over the hardened ice cream, ensuring that it is completely covered and that the meringue meets the biscuit base all around the pie. Bake for just 4–5 minutes, until the meringue is lightly browned.

Leave the pie for 5–10 minutes until cool, then return it to the freezer for a further 2–3 hours, until the meringue is firm. Remove the Ice Cream Pie from the freezer about 20 minutes before serving, and serve in slices.

Mile-High Ice-Cream Pie

MISSISSIPPI MUD PIE

This is rich, stylish and bursting with flavour. Fill the biscuit case carefully so that you will achieve

perfectly even layers of coffee and chocolate "mud" when the pie is cut.

Chocolate Ice Cream (use the recipe for Double
Choc Chip on page 30, but don't add the chocolate
chips at the end)
Coffee Ice Cream (use the recipe for Coffee
Cream Pecan on page 25, but leave out the
caramelized pecan nuts)
100 g/3$^{1}/_{2}$ oz butter
225 g/8 oz crushed chocolate digestive biscuits
1 tsp caster sugar
Bittersweet Chocolate Sauce (see page 109)

METHOD ◇ SERVES 8

Prepare the ice creams. Either have them ready to freeze-churn, if making
them fresh, or temper the coffee ice cream if frozen.

Melt the butter, add the biscuit crumbs and sugar off the heat and mix well.
Press the crumbs into a 20 cm/8 in deep sandwich tin with a removable base,
to coat the base and the sides of the pan. Chill until required.

Freeze-churn the coffee ice cream, or beat the tempered ice cream until
smooth. Half-fill the biscuit case with the ice cream, then freeze for at least 30
minutes. Prepare the chocolate ice cream, then spread it in an even layer over
the hardened coffee ice cream. Freeze the pie for at least a further one hour
before serving.

To make cutting the pie as easy as possible, I recommend allowing it to soften
in the refrigerator for 30 minutes before serving, and slipping it out of the tin
as soon as possible. Spread the pie with the cooled sauce about 5 minutes
before serving.

PEACH MELBA

One of the simplest but most popular of all ice-cream desserts. Its success depends on the ripeness of the peaches,

the flavour of the sauce and the creaminess of the vanilla ice cream.

There are Peach Melbas and desserts that would like to be—this is the real thing!

INGREDIENTS

Raspberry Sauce

125 g/4¹/₂ oz raspberries

half a lemon, grated rind and 1 tsp juice

75 g/2³/₄ oz caster sugar

2 ripe peaches

4 scoops Extra-Rich Vanilla Ice Cream (see page 21)

wafers or piroulines to serve

METHOD ◇ SERVES 2

Whizz the raspberries with the lemon rind and juice and sugar in a food processor or liquidizer until smooth. Press the fruit through a sieve to remove the seeds, then chill the sauce until required.

Cover the peaches with boiling water and leave for no longer than one minute. Slip off the skins, starting from the flower end of the fruit (not the stalk end). Dip the peaches in iced water to refresh them, then cut in half and remove the stones.

Arrange the ice cream scoops and peach halves in a glass or a dish; an enormous champagne glass or a bonbonière is ideal. Decorate with wafers or piroulines (cigarette-shaped wafer-biscuits), then spoon the Raspberry Sauce over the top.

TOOTI FRUITI BOMBE

A bombe is a colourful and impressive dessert, but the flavours and textures of the various sorbets must be chosen with care. Use whatever you have in the freezer, but don't be tempted to mix fruit flavours with the richness of coffee or chocolate; the stronger flavours would just swamp the others.

INGREDIENTS

Strawberry & Kiwi Fruit Sorbet (see page 46)

Honeydew Melon Sorbet (see page 55)

Papaya Lime Sorbet (see page 44)

Pina Colada Sherbet (see page 63)

whipped cream and fresh fruits to decorate

METHOD ◇ SERVES 8−10

Bombes are best made in a round bombe mould, or a round-based metal bowl. Fancy moulds that will turn desserts out in impressive, and often architectural, shapes are not really suitable for ice creams. However, loaf tins or small, round casserole dishes can be used; tins work better than glass bowls since the mixture will freeze more quickly and easily, and stay in shape better. The layers may be arranged in "stripes" across, or moulded to follow the contours of the tin.

Chill a 1.2 litre/2 pint mould in the freezer for at least 2 hours. If you are using sherbets and sorbets (or ice creams) that are already in your freezer, each should be tempered for about 15 minutes before being spooned into the bombe mould.

Press the Strawberry Kiwi Fruit Sorbet into a layer around the sides of the bombe mould, then freeze for 30 minutes until hardened. Remove the Honeydew Melon Sorbet to temper. Mix the sorbet with a fork until smooth, then press a layer over the Strawberry Kiwi Fruit. Return the bombe to the freezer for 30 minutes, and remove the Papaya Lime Sorbet to soften.

Continue building up the layers, mixing the sorbets and sherbets until smooth before spooning them into the tin. Do not overfill the tin with any one layer; even small amounts of ice cream are useful to have in the freezer for one or two people to enjoy.

Chill the finished bombe for at least 2 hours. Soften slightly—for just 10–15 minutes—before serving. You may like to turn the bombe out before your guests arrive, and then return it to the freezer until required. Dip the tin into very hot water for just 10–15 seconds, loosen the bombe and then invert the tin on a serving plate. Give a sharp shake, and the bombe should come out.

Decorate the bombe with whipped cream and fresh fruits before serving.

desserts

Tooti Fruiti Bombe

CHOCOLATE ICE CREAM ROULADE

A luxurious homemade ice-cream dessert with the ice cream of your choice wrapped in a light chocolate and hazelnut sponge. I have suggested using Ginger Ice Cream and Mango Sauce, but you can use your culinary flair to invent the dessert of your dreams.

INGREDIENTS

Ginger Ice Cream (see page 28)

4 large eggs

125 g/4½ oz caster sugar

75 g/2¾ oz toasted ground hazelnuts

1 tsp baking powder, sieved

Mango Sauce (see page 113)

METHOD ◇ SERVES 8

If you are making a fresh batch of ice cream, prepare it to the stage where it is ready to churn, then chill the mixture.

Preheat an oven to 400˚F, then butter and line a jelly roll pan, 12 x 8in, with non-stick baking parchment. Whisk the eggs and sugar until pale and thick; you should be able to trail a number 8 in the mixture when it is ready. Fold in the toasted hazelnuts and baking powder, then lightly spread the mixture into the prepared pan. Bake for 15 minutes, then carefully lift the cake out of the pan, using the baking parchment, to cool on a wire rack.

Soften the ice cream, if previously frozen, for 20 minutes at room temperature. Beat until smooth, then return it to the freezer until required.

Place a piece of baking parchment dredged in powdered sugar on the work surface, and turn the cake out onto it. Remove the parchment it was cooked in, then trim away the edges of the sponge. Spoon the ice cream lengthways into the center of the sponge, taking it right to the shorter edges of the cake. Attention to detail here saves fights later on! Roll up the roulade, enclosing the ice cream in the sponge.

Harden the roulade in the freezer for at least 30 minutes before serving. If you leave it for much longer, you will need to soften the ice cream again for 10–15 minutes at room temperature before serving.

Serve the roulade sliced, with the Mango Sauce spooned around it.

HOOLIGAN'S SOUP

I like whisky in this ice-cream drink, which possibly makes it a Dom Pedro, but Hooligan's Soup is such a

wonderful name! An excellent end to a meal when you are really too full for a dessert. You can decorate this

drink as much as you like, but it should be imbibed through a thick, fun straw.

INGREDIENTS

3 generous scoops Vanilla or
Extra-Rich Vanilla (see pages 20–21) Ice Cream
250 ml/9 fl oz single cream or milk
whisky, as much as you dare
orange slices to decorate

METHOD ◇ SERVES 2

Place all the ingredients in a food processor or liquidizer, and whizz until it is a thick, smooth, drinkable delight. Add a little milk (or whisky), if necessary, or you could add some orange juice. Pour into tall glasses, decorate with orange slices, then serve with a straw.

ACKNOWLEDGEMENTS

The Publishers would like to thank the following for their help in the production of this book:

Mr Martin Bates of
Robotcoup UK Ltd
2 Fleming Way,
Isleworth TW7 6EU
for the provision of the Robotcoup ice cream maker, enabling production of large quantities of ice cream for food styling and photography;

Mr Raj Beedle of
Platignum Homewares
Crown House
Mile Cross Road
Halifax HX1 4HN
for generously providing the Gaggia Gelatiera ice cream machine for recipe testing;

Magimix (UK) Limited,
115a High Street,
Godalming, Surrey GU7 1AQ
for providing two Magimix Gelato Chef 2000 machines for recipe testing;

Moulinex Swan Holdings,
Moulinex Swan House
Albion Street
Birmingham B1 3DL
for providing a Moulinex Gelati Ice Cream maker for the testing of recipes and for photography;

and too
Victor Zaborsky of the International Ice Cream Association, NW Washington DC 20005; **Williams-Sonoma**, New York and San Francisco; **Barry Wilson, editor of Dairy Industry Newletter**, Cambridge; and **Marjie Lambert**, Fort Lauderdale, *for invaluable information and advice.*

index